Praise for *Spark Change*

"From the very first question Jennie asks us in this brilliant book, I was absolutely hooked. Her light-hearted approach and curious process lives up to its promise—to spark the lasting change we seek. This book is a new favorite."

AMY B. SCHER
author of *How to Heal Yourself When No One Else Can*

"The questions in *Spark Change* allow us to mine our own interiors—by leaning into our discomfort, challenging our assumptions, and washing our eyes, we can develop a mind that is more open and a spirit that is more resilient. The book illustrates how we can probe new possibilities and see the future as more fruitful and free, sparking positive change in our bodies, minds, and relationships."

MAYA SOETORO-NG, PHD
Obama Foundation Peace Educator

"In *Spark Change*, Jennie Lee guides the reader through a series of 108 provocative questions that inspire the type of meaningful self-inquiry that can facilitate actual transformation. If our practice is lived 24 hours a day, Jennie offers thought-provoking prompts to impact every minute of those 24 hours. This must-have book is one to be read again and again, used for journaling and discussion with friends, family, and fellow seekers, to set the tone for a life lived with meaning."

FELICIA TOMASKO
editor in chief of *LA YOGA* magazine

"This lovely volume by Jennie Lee reminds us of our capacity—our calling—to explore, to ask questions, to open our hearts and minds to new possibilities. The book guides us gently through self-exploration that leads to renewal and growth. It guides us gently toward discerning where we might be stuck, where we might rob ourselves of opportunity, and where we might find greater fulfillment and joy. This is a must-read and must-use for anyone committed to living even more fully tomorrow than today."

CHRISTIANE BREMS, PHD
clinical professor and director of YogaX at Stanford University; ABPP, E-RYT500, C-IAYT

"This book has a nice balance of asking one to look at the hard questions in life and also how to see new vistas and what is possible. It alternates between looking at the ways we are not serving our higher self and creating a deep sense of self-connection. Both are necessary for healing and transformation."

AMY WHEELER, PHD
President of the International Association of Yoga Therapists

"It is inevitable when a person embarks on a spiritual journey that they will find themselves needing to reflect and re-chart their course as they seek higher ground. This demands the willingness to look clearly and with an open heart in order to navigate toward our greater good and highest joys. We must stop to ask ourselves the very questions that Jennie Lee offers in this powerful guide to help us along our journey. The questions are insightful, evocative, and carry a depth of raw introspection beyond any standard list of questioning. They also do not leave you hanging. She offers the open hand and loving heart to support you as you take your dive inside. Jennie Lee is one of the most supportive, loving, and knowledgeable guides available to us. This book is a true treasure."

"If you want to *be* the change you want to *see*, *Spark Change* is your guide—filled with timeless truth and questions that will take you to greater clarity and fulfillment."

"Step into your best self—*Spark Change* will inspire, challenge, and guide you there."

SPARK
CHANGE

ALSO BY JENNIE LEE

*True Yoga: Practicing with the Yoga Sutras
for Happiness & Spiritual Fulfillment*
(USA Best Book Awards 2016 finalist in
Spirituality: Inspirational category)

Breathing Love: Meditation in Action
(American Book Fest Best Book Awards
2018 Winner: Self Help/Motivational)

SPARK

108 PROVOCATIVE QUESTIONS

CHANGE

FOR SPIRITUAL EVOLUTION

JENNIE LEE

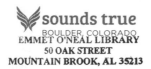

sounds true
BOULDER, COLORADO

158.1

Sounds True
Boulder, CO 80306

Published 2020

Cover and book design by Lisa Kerans

Printed in the United States of America

Library of Congress Cataloging-in-Publication Data

Names: Lee, Jennie, 1965– author.
Title: Spark change: 108 provocative questions for spiritual evolution /
   Jennie Lee.
Description: Boulder: Sounds True, Inc., 2020. | Includes bibliographical
   references.
Identifiers: LCCN 2019048398 (print) | LCCN 2019048399 (ebook) |
   ISBN 9781683644583 (hardcover) | ISBN 9781683644590 (ebook)
Subjects: LCSH: Self-actualization (Psychology) | Spiritual life.
Classification: LCC BF637.S4 L4164 2020   (print) | LCC BF637.S4
   (ebook) | DDC 158.1—dc23
LC record available at https://lccn.loc.gov/2019048398
LC ebook record available at https://lccn.loc.gov/2019048399

10 9 8 7 6 5 4 3 2 1

TO BENEN

May the force of love guide you
through a life of great questions!

The important thing
is not to stop questioning.

ALBERT EINSTEIN

CONTENTS

CHAPTER TWO: VALUES

CHAPTER THREE: BELIEFS

CHAPTER SIX: ACCOUNTABILITY 71

CHAPTER SEVEN: ACCEPTANCE 83

CHAPTER EIGHT: INSPIRATION 95

CHAPTER NINE: KNOWING 107

CHAPTER TEN: LOVE 119

CHAPTER TWELVE: MASTERY

INTRODUCTION

There is a moment when we know that we are ready for *more*—a deeper understanding of life, a more profound experience of it. No one can make us ready, and no one can stop us once this desire awakens within us. There comes an urgency prompted by our soul, a need to know, a need to evolve, a need to *be* more. Sometimes it comes through the proverbial dark night of the soul, and sometimes it just keeps us up at night! As I write this, it's 2:21 a.m.

The urgency to serve this new level of knowing and being is undeniable. It is an unmistakable call to action, and it often begins with a question. For two decades, as I have studied and taught spiritual philosophy and soulful living, one question has burned in my soul, calling me to action again and again. The question is, "How do I keep the flame of personal evolution toward love alive in my heart and how do I ignite the spark of spiritual awakening in others?" Okay that's two questions, but they run together in my mind. The need to serve our shared spiritual advancement is the passion that fuels my life and my work.

The answer I have found, through hundreds of client sessions, conversations with friends, and much internal searching, is that evolution and the willingness to grow mentally, emotionally, and spiritually comes either as a result of dramatic pain and suffering or through the blessing of love. Once this directive from our soul has been ignited, it is painful to try to ignore it. Fortunately, when we give our full attention to personal evolution, it becomes a rock-solid foundation for our happiness.

If this makes sense to you, keep reading, but prepare yourself. Most people want simple answers and an easy button. This book has complex questions and a reality check. There is *no* easy button to spiritual self-awareness. It is a process that requires a ruthless willingness to introspect and undaunted courage to change that which needs changing. No one can do the work for you. But this book can help you do it, if you are awake, and if you are ready. Herein lies an invitation to know yourself better, accept yourself more, and realize your life's highest potentials.

This is the work I do with my yoga therapy clients. Rather than offer advice, I ask illuminating questions that help them find their own inner truth. Then I share practices that enable them to maintain and live from that soul-connected place. I have seen brilliant transformation in every category of people's lives as a result of this process, from deepened relationships to improved health and newfound purpose. Sadly, I have also watched people pay good money to get the map and the equipment and then never take the journey.

THE VALUE OF INTROSPECTION

Through years of coaching, I have learned that telling someone what to do, or even how to do it, is not enough. Asking the right questions is what matters, because by trying to answer them, people become invested in their own solutions and ways to change. Inquiry is necessary to every human life. From the time we learn to speak, we question the world around us and our experiences within it. Only humans have a consciousness that can observe and analyze itself and make choices based on its conscience.

The questions in this book will help you cultivate greater self-knowing and eventually self-actualization, which leads to an unshakeable inner happiness that is the bedrock of true success. The purpose of the questions is to engage you in the practice of introspection. By puzzling through the right question at the right time, you click on the creative brain and fuel yourself with intention. As you solve your own quandaries, you expand your consciousness and level of joy. As Socrates said, "the unexamined life is not worth living."

WHAT IF . . .

Imagine for a moment that life has a question for you. Are you listening to what it is asking right now? Are you aware of your soul's intention for embodiment at this time or are you at odds with it? By taking a break from the restless rush of life to ponder such questions and to listen to your inner spirit, you give yourself an exceptional gift and consciously invoke your personal evolution.

Introspection such as this book suggests is not for the fainthearted or the self-critical. It is essential to cultivate a positive relationship with our own minds, assessing whether the thoughts and questions we are entertaining are helpful for our development or not; whether they are life-affirming or detrimental to our spirit. We must be able to raise difficult questions without falling prey to the negative or judgmental inner critic. In order to do this, self-inquiry requires courage, self-compassion, and ridiculous amounts of humor. When undertaken in the right way, it enables us to relax into our lives, as we come to understand and embrace both the absurdity and the lovability of our human nature.

MORE ON WHY QUESTIONS MATTER

Our whole internal thinking process operates on a question-and-answer, or Q and A, system, so it stands to reason that if we are seeking new solutions to life's challenges, it behooves us to make this Q and A dialogue in our heads conscious. Quality questions lead to quality answers. Good friends, good parents, and good leaders all know that the right questions are like keys to our inner doors. They take us to something within that we don't yet know or haven't yet considered. They give us a new way of looking at problems. That is why questions form the foundation of introspection. To be able to question ourselves and life shows curiosity and a willingness to grow. Questions promote deeper thought, connection, authenticity, and humility. They gnaw at us and push us toward greater clarity. And they spark wonder.

Introspection helps us create a thematic, narrative thread for our lives, keeping us on track and nudging us into new possibilities. It is a daily conscious effort to improve ourselves and spiritualize our lives. Good questions help us move toward the intentional creation of our desires and illuminate what sets us backward into old, unconscious patterning or habitual reactivity.

As we learn to be authentic in the questions we ask ourselves, we simultaneously learn how to engage others with connection-building questions as well. This deepens our relationships by engendering empathy, compassion, and understanding. The more truthful we become in our self-reflection process, the more we will recognize any hidden motivations for asking certain questions of others. We will see if we are leading them toward an answer we hope to receive, creating a distraction so we don't have to be vulnerable, or trying to expose some weakness of theirs in order to feel better about ourselves. As we learn to ask questions that uplift and inspire, we experience greater harmony and love, in our own hearts and in every external relationship. And eventually, in addition to evolving into greater self-awareness, we also evolve beyond it to self-transcendence and the expanded experience of oneness.

WHAT TO EXPECT FROM THE QUESTIONS

When I meet someone who asks powerhouse questions, I tingle with joy. Feeling stopped, in need of a moment to ponder my answer, I know I am on the edge of a new perspective and a liberating possibility. In these pages, I aspire to be one of these people for you. I hope these questions make you stop and really think. I encourage you to look at the questions you are asking of life and to listen to the questions life is asking of you. I believe that by undertaking an intentional approach to the questions we ask of ourselves and each other, we will make quicker evolutionary strides, individually and collectively.

I chose 108 questions because the number 108 is significant in many world religions, as well as in fields such as science, literature, technology, and yogic philosophy. On a *mala*, the strand of beads used for repeating mantras, there are typically 108 beads.

In Hinduism, there are 108 Upanishads, which are sacred texts of the ancient sages, and 108 names for God. The number 108 is a Harshad number, an integer divisible by the sum of its digits. *Harshad* is a Sanskrit word meaning "giver of joy." There are 54 letters in the Sanskrit alphabet, and each has masculine (*shiva*) and feminine (*shakti*) forms: 54 × 2 = 108. There are said to be 108 earthly desires, 108 lies that humans tell, and 108 human delusions or forms of ignorance. It has been proposed that if one can be so calm in meditation as to have only 108 breaths in a day, enlightenment will come. And finally, 1 stands for highest truth, 0 for the emptying of the ego into complete spiritual practice, and 8 for the infinite or eternal soul.

The 108 questions are divided into twelve major themes—one theme for each chapter—and each theme has nine questions. Each question is followed by an explanation of its significance and instructions for how to engage with it more deeply. You may decide to take the themes in order and consider one per month for a year or dip into whatever subject strikes your interest, exploring each as it pertains to your life. Some questions may seem similar but are actually another layer of exploration on a particular topic.

THE POWER OF GREAT QUESTIONS

In preparation for this book, I reviewed the personal journals I have kept over the past forty years. I saw repeated examples of how my inner questioning led to my greatest growth. This is why I believe so strongly in the power of introspective questions to lead us all into our full evolutionary potential. The very answer to my nagging question, "How do I keep the flame of personal evolution toward love alive in my heart and how do I ignite the spark of spiritual awakening in others?" lies in the continual asking of deeper questions.

For the past two decades in my yoga therapy practice, I have counseled people seeking greater self-awareness as they navigate experiences such as depression, grief, and stress. Regardless of presenting issues, every person has come because they want to feel happier, more at peace with themselves and the world they live in, and more able to cope with life's challenges. They seek a deeper meaning and purpose in life and a connection to their soul and to the transcendent energy of life itself. This is the driving force beneath all the things we call "self-help."

The questions I offer have come from my own inner journey as well as my study of the philosophies and practices of classical yoga, as taught by spiritual masters such as Paramahansa Yogananda and Mata Amritanandamayi, and the principles of spiritual psychology, as expressed by teachers such as Gary Zukav, Carl Rogers, and Eckhart Tolle. By working through the 108 questions you will learn to listen deeply to your soul and determine what life is calling for you to learn or to express.

In his *Letters to a Young Poet*, Rainer Maria Rilke wrote, "Be patient toward all that is unsolved in your heart and try to love the questions themselves, like locked rooms and like books that are written in a very foreign tongue. . . . Live the questions now. Perhaps you will then gradually, without noticing it, live along some distant day into the answer."

TIPS FOR WORKING WITH THE QUESTIONS

Your spiritual development depends on how well you can apply your answers to these questions in daily life. To truly benefit from them, you must take time to let the material become a part of you. It is not enough to just read through them. Like chewing food thoroughly in order to digest it properly, we assimilate the wisdom these questions provide by taking time to fully absorb each one. There is no rush. Allow time for assimilation. Concentrate on one question until it feels complete in your mind and heart. Don't get indigestion by flooding yourself with too many unresolved questions at once.

Before beginning, set aside a few moments of silence. Just as white space on a page creates a sense of spaciousness for words, silence allows space for the meaning of each question to percolate in your mind. When you feel ready, read a question and then repeat it several times silently.

After you have pondered your answer for a while, make some notes. Write down any associated thoughts, connections, insights, or follow-up questions. You may even try writing the question out, as this will help your mind bring in your right answer. Life moves into manifestation from our minds through our hands. The synchronicity created by directing pen across paper activates parts of the brain associated with both thinking and memory. Writing answers out by hand will help you go deeper into your truth and will solidify it in your subconscious mind, which influences future choices and behaviors.

Don't censor your answers and don't worry about grammar or writing style. This is just for you and there is no right or wrong way to write your answers. If you get stuck on a question, you do not need to feel inadequate to it, just recognize that it requires patience and the willingness to look deeper. Try rewording it in a way that makes more sense to you. If any fear arises, it is probably related to not having the answers immediately. No problem! Your journal is your personal space of exploration. Be honest, fearless, and unfiltered. Trust your internal process.

Some questions may challenge you or trigger a negative response, like this one did for me: "What am I supposed to learn from this (situation, difficult relationship, etc.)?" For over a decade, whenever I considered this, I would groan and roll my eyes because I knew what was coming: a deep dive into my own responsibility for said situation or relational conflict. Ugh! I just wanted to blame others or hide and try to avoid the drama altogether. But it is the questions that we loathe and resist that are often the ones we benefit from the most. If you run across questions that feel troublesome, try reframing them slightly, like modifying a yoga posture you have difficulty with, in order to honor your body. If this doesn't work, move on, but consider coming back to revisit them later. If two questions seem similar, look carefully for subtle differences and nuances.

Take note of any of your own questions that arise as you ponder the ones presented here. Watch how you phrase your internal questions and be careful of ones like "Why has this happened to me?" or "Why is life so hard?" which keep you disempowered. Take a position of control and reframe them to something like, "How can I grow through what has happened to me?" or "How am I self-sabotaging?" In this way, you will move quickly toward truth and the ability to make necessary personal changes.

You may want to share any particularly meaningful questions with a trusted friend to stimulate conversation. Definitely carry your favorites with you and practice active reflection in order to embody your answers. A consistent habit of introspection will reap great benefits of personal growth, well-being, and joy. Most importantly, enjoy the new perspectives that the questions offer, and even if only one question touches your heart, consider that a success.

So, go grab a pen, make some tea, and settle in. I hope you will enjoy the 108 questions as much as I have. Please know that every one of them is offered in a spirit of love and the hope that it will take you to the remembrance of your beautiful soul. Now, if you are awake and ready, it's time to find out what more life has for you!

CHAPTER ONE

CHANGES

Humans are wired for homeostasis. We resist change. Even when we *want* things to be different, we often don't *do* anything to change, because the known feels better than the unknown. So, we keep ourselves stuck.

Most people love to complain. Bonding through our rants, we vent about problems far more than we brainstorm solutions. Trapped inside negative patterns of thinking and righteous defense of our opinions, we waste precious time that could be better spent getting to know our beautiful souls and manifesting a more harmonious life. Although freedom from this limited state of being is just one new thought away, change for most people is as terrifying as skydiving without a chute.

It takes a fair amount of faith to risk change. If we are not sure it will be worth the effort, we often decide to just leave well enough alone. We avoid it because change seems, and often is, difficult. It requires sacrifice, and no one likes loss or lack. Change demands strength, and because we are often weak-willed, we default to what is familiar, even if it is unhealthy or sometimes downright destructive.

However, the ultimate reason we evade change is because we identify with our limited bodies and personalities (i.e., the ego self) and this separate, scared part of who we are tries to maintain the status quo at all cost. If we have not made friends with, or learned to trust, our expansive spiritual Self, we will feel unsupported by life. But really, every soul carries a cosmic chute waiting to be released *when* we have the courage to rip the cord of old thought, shift into a new perspective, and embrace change.

To begin this kind of intentional, positive change, consider where you feel stuck right now; maybe in interpersonal conflict, career ambivalence, self-judgment, or fear. You have a choice: stay there for an indefinite amount of wasted time or inch your way to the open door and get ready to launch into a conscious and exhilarating ride through life. Your spiritual essence cannot be ignored forever, and the beautiful secret is that as soon as you leap, you realize just how limitless you have always been.

The process of conscious change, and how to initiate, accomplish, and sustain it for the purpose of our spiritual evolution, is where we begin the questions. The ability to question oneself is fundamental to personal growth. Like Albert Einstein proposed, if we have an hour to solve a problem and our lives depended on the solution, we should spend the first fifty-five minutes determining the proper question to ask, for once we know that, we can usually solve the problem in less than five minutes.

How many times does something have to happen before it occurs to me to change?

If you are stuck or dissatisfied with life in some way, or if you recognize a recurring pattern of frustration, notice how you feel about change in general. Ambivalent? Resistant? Afraid? You can be all of these and still move forward. If you have had enough of the same results and are ready to create a different experience, tell yourself that it is time to face fear and act anyway. You can always ask for help. In fact, please *do* ask for help. Don't wait for the wake-up call to be so extreme that help is no longer available. Ask now and be willing to accept help when it is offered.

Take a moment and feel the place within your heart that is more than ready for a new experience in life. Notice the sensation of constriction that staying stuck in old patterns causes and then breathe some space around it gently. The basic requirements for change are as follows:

- Recognize the need for it.

- Believe it is possible.

- Want it badly enough to do the work required.

- Be willing to move through any fear that arises.

- Ask for help if needed.

- Be patient and self-compassionate.

- Surrender attachment to a specific outcome.

What needs to change in my life right now?

Don't give this question a lot of thought. The first thing that comes to mind is the one you should focus on first. It is most likely what your gut knows needs changing, but that you've been actively avoiding. If you thought, "Everything!" pause and take a deep breath. Get as quiet as you can and then ask again, "What's the *first* thing that needs to change in my life right *now*?" Trust your answer.

If by chance you draw a complete blank, take a short walk without headphones or a telephone. Just walk and allow your mind to wander, absorbing the environment around you. A clue will usually surface. Give yourself some time to fully imagine a new reality. If nothing arises, move on to the next question, which should help you get clarity. And if you have a long-held need for change in a certain area of your life, pay close attention to the next question as well.

What am I resisting and what is the resistance telling me?

Think about the ways in which you avoid change. Maybe there are things you have known needed changing for months, years, or for as long as you can remember. Your on-going resistance to positive change is telling you something. And that is, there is an even greater need beneath the one you have identified. So, what is it? What do you need even more than the change you first identified? For instance, maybe you have a resistance to exercise, even though you know you need it. But you notice that what you need even more is rest, physical and/or mental. Adding one more thing to do (exercise) therefore feels burdensome. If you allowed yourself the rest that your body and mind are craving, then you may move into a natural rhythm of exercise with ease.

Consider all the ways in which you disallow your true needs. Then step outside of yourself for a moment and try to look at your life as if you were a dear friend. See your current situation from that friend's point of view and listen to what they might tell you. Changing perspective will give you new ideas. This a great practice in what is called witnessing, or disidentifying with the experience itself in order to claim peace and equanimity, and it is also a wonderful way to recognize the myriad of possibilities that exist for you in any given moment.

What do I fear would happen if I made the change I need to make?

All change upsets the status quo, at least temporarily. Fearing this, we often avoid the temporary discomfort that comes before long-term gain. When we know we need to change something but haven't, we must clarify our underlying fears and look carefully at the perceived benefit of staying stuck. To avoid responsibility for change keeps us in inner turmoil, and this inner conflict creates anxiety. The longer we stay in it, the more chronic our suffering becomes.

No one can make change for you and no one can make you change. All of your fence-sitting is just time (i.e., life) being wasted. Like opening a window for fresh spring air to waft in after being closed all winter, when you initiate pro-active change, you introduce new possibility. If you do not, you breed unrest by remaining incongruent, internally at odds with yourself. This kind of stagnancy brings unhappiness and death, if not to your body, at least to your spirit. To get out of the stuck place, rewrite your internal script by replacing all self-negating thoughts with compassionate, affirmative ones. You intuitively know what needs to change. And you know that no one but you can change it. So, move. Do something, literally anything, to begin building the momentum.

How do I consistently lie to myself?

One of the primary ways in which people excuse themselves from making change is through the lies they tell themselves: "I'll do it when I have more time . . . when I feel calmer . . . when there is less going on . . ." Blah, blah, blah. We know when we are lying to ourselves, and excuses get us only to where we currently are. Lying serves nothing, certainly not your well-being.

If you have recognized a need for change, stop procrastinating by lying to yourself. You won't do it tomorrow. You won't have more time a month from now. And there certainly won't be less stress anytime soon in this crazy world. Not to mention that you won't feel calmer unless you make the necessary changes your life is calling for. Freedom comes with the refusal to hide. Write down the greatest lie you tell yourself right now. If there is more than one, make a list. Get these toxins out of your system today.

Do I set self-honoring boundaries?

Change will never happen if we have no energy to devote to it. For this reason, many people skirt change by staying too busy for it, overgiving to others and neglecting their own needs. However, if this goes on indefinitely and we do not set appropriate, self-honoring boundaries, we will eventually become resentful. And if that isn't enough, we might even fall ill, in a subconscious attempt to claim our much-needed personal time. This is not the way to approach change.

Get in the habit of daily relaxation. Manage tension levels through muscular relaxation and mental surrender. Be sure to leave some energy at the end of the day to meditate, even for five to ten minutes. By creating space for yourself to rest, and accepting where you are right now, you will sustain the energy and availability to hear the life-changing messages your soul sends out.

When I made a positive change in the past, how did I do it?

We have all moved through challenges at some point. Looking back to recognize the strength we developed through our trials, we can consciously call upon it now or in the future. There are many strategies we may have employed in order to cope with difficulty. Journaling, therapy, time with trusted friends, time alone in nature, physical movement like yoga, energy balancing such as Reiki, or massage are just some of the ways people regain equilibrium after a trauma or loss. Tears shed freely are always healing and time does its work on us, too.

Consider a difficult experience you have lived through and what skills or strategies you drew upon. Maybe a desired relationship ended, but rather than spend time in anger or self-judgment, you determined to be bigger than the loss. You gave it meaning by taking the opportunity to embody the qualities you missed in the other person. By cultivating more inner balance, you saw how the challenge prepared you for new relationships in the future. You overcame the challenge consciously and stepped into a greater level of awareness and strength. You carry these forward into future desired changes.

How could I be more integrated in body and mind?

Life changes when we change how we live. Through all our choices and actions, we create our destiny. Self-actualization is the process of consciously choosing the highest and best ways to become our most congruent self. To do this we need body, mind, and spirit all on the same team. Sometimes the body acts from habit, not honoring what the spirit knows to be our best path. Other times the mind pushes the body in ways the body knows is not self-honoring.

Begin to pay attention to every choice, big and small. Watch how you may go with the expected choice or the seemingly appropriate one, even if it doesn't really fit you. Or maybe you consistently show up as less than your best self, thereby diminishing your life until you are trapped in self-loathing, depression, or numbness. Even if you are too tired or discouraged to take big action, make an intentional, graceful choice for your health, truth, and integration today. One tiny movement, one positive thought, chosen with the intention to align yourself in body, mind, and soul begins to shift things. In doing this, you build the strength and resilience to live *your* life.

What question am
I afraid to ask?

This may seem like a conundrum, especially in a book of questions. How can we know what we do not know? But as we look at our fear, we will certainly see places where we are choosing the safe rather than the creative, the stifling known rather than the liberating unknown. We can't be faulted for choices made in times of lesser awareness, but once we know that we are choosing against ourselves, it becomes critical for our well-being to discipline our mental processes in order to follow a healthy path to congruency within.

If there is a question you are afraid to face, try asking it of a few friends or family members first. Then take yourself and that pesky question on a date and woo it out of the shadows. Let it tell you what needs to be answered. When you feel clearer, give yourself a reward for being brave.

CHAPTER TWO

VALUES

Our values define who we are, and they set the course for our lives. If we do not clarify what our core values are, we can be certain of uncertainty, a constantly wavering path. But when we establish ourselves in what represents our highest and best, we create a strong foundation for all of our decisions and a stable reference point from which to move forward.

When we are sure of our highest commitments, anchored in our values, we discern whether an activity or relationship is bringing us closer to integration or further away. We know what is vital for the well-being of our spirit and become more organized with our goals, and the use of our energy and time. We see what is working in our lives, and what is not, and we are able to identify distractions and clear complications with ease.

If you have never considered what your true values are, or if it feels a bit frightening to do so, you are not alone. Some people stay in confusion, subconsciously seeing un-intentionality as safety, or calling it spontaneity. Their lack of compulsion to act becomes a self-written permission slip for inaction. But to remain undeclared is not to remain fluid so much as to remain deeply unsatisfied. Until we live in a way that honors what we truly value, we are fragmented and will stumble repeatedly into wrong choices. Misaligned, we crave outer directives, looking to other people to make us feel alive rather than sourcing energy and assurance from within. In doing this, we diminish ourselves and squander our precious life force.

By clarifying your personal values and priorities, you will then know what you need to maintain balance and move forward. Clear values help you get out of your own way as you determine your purpose and chart your course of inspired action. By boldly living your truth, you will become stronger, more self-sufficient, and more joyful. And you will fortify your self-esteem and self-respect.

In chapter 4, we examine willingness and willpower, two strengths that require clearly defined core values. The willingness to initiate change can only come when we feel genuinely aligned with our deepest truth. And the determination to live according to our ideals requires willpower, the ability to control our thoughts, attitudes, and behaviors, especially when things are challenging or an easier path tempts us.

Consider for a moment what questions you have been asked lately and the values they indicate about the person asking. Someone may have wanted to know who you have studied with or what books you have read, showing a value for intellectual pursuits. Someone else may have been more interested in your life experiences and how they have shaped your inner being. This shows a value for matters of the heart and personal resiliency.

Think about what questions you typically ask yourself and others, and what they reveal about your values. Or if you are not one to ask many questions, note how this also says something distinct about your values. Then dive into the following questions to clarify your values even further.

What do I prioritize on a daily basis?

People generally do what they *want* to do. Our choices clearly illustrate our priorities, which are a direct reflection of our values. All of our choices serve us in some way, even the choice of avoidance. When you decide to live from clearly chosen values, you can no longer hide. Contradictions hamper your well-being.

Begin by making a list of the activities and people you prioritize on a regular basis. Think about how these choices reflect certain core values. You are giving precious time and energy to them, so if there is a discrepancy between what you are prioritizing and what you truly value, it is time for some restructuring. Assess why this discrepancy exists. Usually it is because you have not clarified your values, or there is a sense of "have to" or "should" regarding the prioritized activities. Remember that you have the power of choice. Replace any "have to's" and "shoulds" with "coulds" instead, and notice if you would be doing the same things or something different. Be intentional about how you use your creative energy.

What do my possessions say about my prevailing values?

Take an honest assessment of your physical environment. You will quickly see certain values exhibited through the excess or lack of material items, as well as the quality of what you possess. Imagine someone you didn't know, from a foreign land, walking into your home. What would they see about your values?

Now, imagine that a natural disaster was about to occur, and you had to flee taking only ten things with you. This exercise will help you to quickly identify what holds the greatest significance for you. Notice if there are any surprises on the list. Determine the consistent meaning or value represented by the items you chose. Finally, assess whether your current living environment and possessions accurately reflect your true values. Notice things in your home you may like to get rid of and the qualities these exemplify. By keeping them, you are supporting that value. If you were to get rid of them that would support a different value. If the majority of possessions you have do not reflect what is of greatest value to you, it is time to start clearing house. Everything you own, small and large, is a symbol of your prevailing values.

When do I feel
best about myself?

Imagine stepping outside your life for a moment and watching it like a movie. There are scenes in which you are happy and thriving and scenes in which you are stagnant and unfulfilled. Notice details about the people, the conversations, and the activities that make you feel good about yourself. There are core values embedded here. Determine what they are. Do the same for the scenes where you don't seem happy. What values are being violated by the choice of how you are spending your time and with whom?

If the character in your movie seems imbalanced, think about what they need to change to become more peaceful in heart and mind. Help your character by rewriting their script so they can focus on what's most important. Start writing that new life now by affirming that you will honor yourself through selecting relationships and activities that support your highest values.

QUESTION 13

What am I
devoted to?

Devotion is the heart's call. It is deeply connected to our most significant values. Unlike regular commitments that sometimes come from obligation, guilt, or sheer discipline, devotion is different. It is infused with love because we are devoted to what we love.

Consider what your heart is calling you to and how this aligns with your core values. Maybe you have been ignoring your heart's messages, but if you hope to live an authentic life, you have to honor this heart wisdom as much as the mind's knowledge. Otherwise your life will be fragmented and based on partial truth. Notice your level of self-trust in this moment and how it corresponds to whether you are living from your heart's true values or not. If you are still unclear about what these are, let love lead you in the right direction. And if you don't feel devoted to anything at this time, try listening more deeply to what your heart needs.

What do I want more of in my life?

We all have certain longings that just never quit. These are the inner whispers for more free time, more money, more help, more creative opportunities, more of something that lights our fire. These longings may flare or recede at times but always there is a nagging, persistent need for *more*. You know what they are, and there is at least one thing you can do to take a step closer to one of them.

Schedule some time for a date with yourself, dedicated to one of your longings. Create a vision board for manifestation. Ask for help from a friend. If money prevents you from pursuing what you want, begin saving even a dollar toward it today. If something else stands in your way, question what deeper or secondary value it represents. And finally, consider whether life is asking you to practice contentment in this moment rather than seeking change. Whatever choice you make, be sure it honors your deepest values.

What are the ten things in my life now that will matter most ten years from now?

After you have made your list, go back to Question 10 and see how many of these activities or people are being prioritized on a daily basis. If few or none are, it may be time to restructure your schedule to honor what is most important. If you could not name ten things, begin imagining what you would like in your life now that would also matter ten years down the road. Give some energy and thought to how these things could be created. If this feels difficult, imagine what would become important if you had less than a year to live.

If you are locked into doing things you don't enjoy, with people who do not enliven you, you are undermining your own integrity, creativity, and life-force energy. Reduce complications, excess commitments, and possessions that serve nothing in terms of core values. The stronger your conviction in aligning with your highest values is, the easier simplification becomes. Reorganize and streamline.

QUESTION 16

What type of person would I like to develop a relationship with?

Both personally and professionally, who you choose to spend time with matters. People can be uplifting, neutral, or negative and as you strive to live from your core values, it is important to choose company that shares the values that uplift you. Notice any differences between what you value in relationships, and what your partner, friends, and colleagues value. If these people are not positive influences, you can create healthy boundaries and limit the time you spend with them. When possible, eliminate the relationships you know you would not miss.

Pay attention to the qualities you admire most in people and consider how you could develop these more within yourself. Invite connection with people who are living the values you aspire to at an even higher level than you currently are. Surround yourself with positive, inspiring people or nurture yourself with alone time until you find a new tribe.

What gives my life the most meaning?

At first glance this may be a beloved person, a creative pursuit, or a mission. Recognize these, but then look a bit deeper at what it is about your relationship with this person or passion that gives you the greatest sense of meaning and purpose. Maybe it is feeling needed or helpful to someone you love. Maybe it is serving the greater good of humanity in some way. Or it could be the joy you feel in sharing your creativity in a unique manner. Define the value you hold in relation to the activity or person.

Consider also the universal values that are esteemed across nations, religions, and philosophies. Foundational to our well-being are practices such as peacefulness, integrity, love, respect, responsibility, fairness, compassion, and right conduct. These values make life more fulfilling and harmonious. Maybe there are new ways you can strive to embody these, or maybe it is time to seek new meaningful pursuits.

At my core,
what do I stand for?

Forget about your outer roles, relationship status, and job title for a moment. Look within to the qualities that make up your inner nature. Are you compassionate, loving, or funny? Every one of us has a core essence, our deepest nature, made up of qualities that were not taught to us but that we have had since birth. Once you know the qualities that form your core, you can create strong inner commitments to yourself and others based on them. Unlike goals that define *what* you want to accomplish in life, inner commitments essentially define *why* you do what you do. Here are some examples:

- I make choices based on love, not fear,
  because I am courageous.

- I practice mindfulness, because I am curious.

- I speak truth with compassion, because I am kind.

Write some of your own inner commitments now, based on who you are at your core. If this is not yet clear, consider what qualities you would *like* to be known for and the ones you hope to embody through your choices. Then try writing a personal mission statement using your top two inner commitments or desired qualities. For example, "I courageously move through my life, practicing truthfulness and lovingkindness in all of my choices and relationships."

CHAPTER THREE

BELIEFS

Once we have defined our values and identified needed changes, then it's time to determine what is required to make these value-honoring transformations a reality. To do this, we must begin at the energetic level, as energy is the basis of everything. Energy is the universal creative force, also known as consciousness moving into manifestation. Energy is activated and directed through thought, our personal instrument of creativity. Every thought points our energy in a certain direction, so it is imperative that we assess whether this creative power is being utilized in life-enhancing ways or detrimental ones.

Recurring thoughts reinforce the energy they hold every time we allow them to play in our minds. By continually thinking in a certain pattern, a belief blueprint is formed in the energetic realm, and a neural pathway is created in the brain. Each time it is repeated, the neural pathway becomes stronger until these thoughts play automatically. Repetitive thoughts create belief habits that directly shape our daily experience.

Because of this energetic principle, our thoughts and beliefs can become either our worst enemies or our best friends. They can limit us or free us. The trend of our thoughts is the most powerful creative force in our lives, and it is essential that we manage it consciously. We become what we repeatedly think and do.

Fortunately, we have the capacity to change our thoughts, beliefs, and yes, our habits too, at any moment, thereby creating change in our life experience. Think of this like a circle: belief drives choice; choice creates experience; experience solidifies belief. And around and around we go. If we ever hope to change our experience, we *must* change our beliefs. It is the only place to interrupt the vicious cycle.

By questioning our beliefs, we liberate ourselves from potential ignorance, mediocrity, and habitual response to a life that is ever-evolving, or should be. Rather than staying mired in self-judgment for our shortcomings or mistakes, we can replace negative traits with their positive opposites: we can exchange fear for courage, dullness for creativity, criticism for self-respect, and stagnation for adaptability to change. By managing our thoughts, we cultivate self-worth, and we feel better. In this way, we take control of our lives.

Some repetitive thought patterns can be subtle, and it often takes years to see the effects they bring. For this reason, we need to be ever-watchful and fill our internal cup with loving, life-affirming thoughts, in order to disable the subconscious saboteurs of habitual beliefs, which throw us off course. By challenging our beliefs and training our consciousness to forgo the momentary ease that a habit might bring, we create lasting success and step into our limitless spiritual expression.

QUESTION 19

Are my thoughts helping
or hurting me?

Just because you have thought or believed something for a long time does not make it true. Refuse to let habitual patterns of thought keep you stuck. Identify the voices in your head that mimic voices from your past, especially ones that were not kind, empowering, or loving. Delete any thoughts that do not support your well-being, as swiftly as you would an offensive email in your inbox. Immediately replace self-defeating thoughts or beliefs with the positive opposite.

Consider the core values you identified in the last chapter and whether your thoughts support them. Only allow ones that honor your values to hold time and space in your mind. Elect a more compassionate, life-affirming inner dialogue and set yourself free. Liberate yourself now with a belief system overhaul. Throw out any recurring thoughts that sabotage you when you consider making change. You are a limitless soul ready to shine.

What belief am I overly attached to?

Sometimes, even when we know that a belief is hurting us, we find ourselves attached to it, like a comfortable yet worn-out sweater. Beliefs are tenacious, and we often hold on to them, even when they have been proven wrong multiple times. Like that sweater taking up precious space in your closet, these beliefs have got to go. In order to release them, first identify what the underlying fear is, what you think will happen if you let go of said belief. Imagine if you were to change this belief, what the worst-case scenario might be. Then imagine the best-case scenario. Maybe this belief is still serving you in some way. If a belief served a purpose in the past, you may subconsciously think that by holding on to it you ensure a certain future as well.

Unfortunately, fear is keeping you attached but deluded. The secure future you want is actually guaranteed with more certainty if you bring yourself completely into this moment with full awareness and courage. Replace outgrown beliefs that create limitation with ones that foster expansive possibility, and exchange activities that distract you from your true desires for ones that support your core values. By changing your thoughts and taking control of your experience, you will move beyond attachment into a fluid adaptability, ready for any necessary changes.

What am I defending?

Whenever a sense of defensiveness arises, it is a call for your attention. Some aspect of you feels threatened. If, in this vulnerable moment, you sit quietly with that tender part that needs to be heard, then you can move out of defense and into understanding of yourself, rather than fighting for understanding from another. This lessens the tension that arises when you feel the need to defend yourself or your position in some way. It fosters self-acceptance and enables you to communicate with greater calm.

Defensiveness is often an attempt to hide our flaws, but it keeps us stuck in self-consciousness and self-involvement. Self-protective choices do not bring happiness, they bring isolation. When you acknowledge the truth behind your fear, you are being courageously authentic. We all hold paradoxes within, and to attempt to appear flawless is to move even further away from wholeness. We have to risk the safety of the familiar to reach new heights of self-awareness. The freedom from defensive habits creates a psychological happiness far more lasting than any material success.

What is my limiting
belief pattern?

The following are a few common limiting beliefs that plague most human beings:

- I am not worthy.

- I am not loveable.

- I am not enough.

- I am not like other people.

- I am alone.

These beliefs inform every aspect of our lives: our education, work, relationships, and health. And the repetition of them solidifies a repeated experience of the same. Look to the patterns in your life, recurring experiences that have happened numerous times in various forms.

Maybe you have been betrayed in multiple ways or abandoned by more than one person. Maybe you have regularly been dismissed or falsely accused. Notice what you believe about these patterns, and you will find your *core* limiting belief. Then assess your own behavior, communication, and defense in these areas. Get out of the self-perpetuating cycle and stop reinforcing the very experiences you seek to eliminate. Try meditation for just a few minutes each day to practice witnessing the repetitive internal loops your mind makes and step out of them for a moment into self-love. Over time, you will distance yourself from these limiting patterns altogether until they are no longer part of who you are.

Why do I believe
___ about myself?

It is important to acknowledge when, where, and why a negative belief about yourself was first established, because these inner conflicts create external situations of frustration. Let's say you notice the belief, "I am not supported." The core limiting belief within this is that the Universe is a place of lack, rather than abundance. Behind the belief of not being supported there may be other beliefs such as, "It is better to be self-sacrificing or self-sufficient than ask for help" or maybe "I don't deserve help." As long as these hold court in your consciousness, fear will fuel the experience of being without support and further lack will fuel more fear. That is until you say "Stop!" and replace the self-limiting beliefs one by one.

Determine what you *want* to experience, and the belief that is needed to achieve your goal. Using the above example, if what you want to experience is support, you could adopt and affirm one or all of the following:

- I live in a loving and abundant Universe that supports me with its infinite resources.

- When I ask for help, I receive it in abundance.

- I am a part of the one consciousness in which I have all that I need.

What is the inner need that my worst habit fulfills?

This reflection is particularly interesting because it helps us see what belief really needs to be addressed. Don't stop with the first obvious answer. Go several layers into the inner needs. There is something being served by holding on to any bad habit. For example, let's say your worst habit is having a nightly drink. The first obvious answer is that it fulfills the need to relax. Going a level deeper, the need to relax is actually a need to create more balance in life between work and self-care. Beneath that is the need to be more self-honoring with your time commitments, acknowledging your needs as equal to those of whom you love and care for. Beneath that is the need to realize your worth regardless of whether you are doing for others. Look at all of the beliefs that go along with the habit.

This habit will repeat until you go to the deepest level of need you identified and choose a new belief to honor that need. In this case, "I am worthy of self-care and life balance." As you embody this truth, then you will find more soul-nourishing ways to honor the original need to relax.

Have I made
unhappiness a habit?

No one can make you happy if you choose to be unhappy. And no one can make you unhappy if you believe you are happy. Period. Happiness is a habit. Unhappiness is a habit. The choice is yours. Ask yourself honestly if you are addicted to unhappiness or moodiness. If you find that you are, the first course of action is to expose your expectations. Most likely the expectations you place on yourself or others are too high. Adjust them to a more realistic level.

Then, as in overcoming any bad habit, it is essential to concentrate on creating the positive opposite. Choose to be courageously cheerful regardless of outer circumstances. Practice smiling and being happy. Determine absolutely that you will not allow the behavior of others to affect your inner peace. Be patient with the process, but be determined. And seek deeper levels of soul joy that go beyond the transitory happiness hits most people focus on. Practice gratitude constantly and focus on giving rather than just serving your own desires.

How can I stay positive in challenging situations?

Even if we actively practice being happy, it's easy to lose ground when challenges arise. When they do, one of the best antidotes to sadness, worry, or fear is simple appreciation, thankfulness for that which is still good. Think, read, and repeat statements of gratitude to clear away negativity. Eliminate all doubt about your capacity to change by insisting on your strength and freedom now. Practice vigilant thought watching and allow no room for negation of any kind. Affirm joyful thoughts with deep concentration, knowing that your ability to change is chiefly determined by the quality of your attention.

A consistently positive outlook and naturally positive habit of thought can be cultivated with the right effort. Start now by writing five positive thoughts. Then write five things you appreciate or are thankful for. As often as possible, reinforce your efforts by spending time with other positive people in soul-nourishing environments. Avoid anything or anyone that undermines your upbeat attitude.

Are my beliefs feeding my ego or my soul?

At any given moment your consciousness may be directed by your ego or your soul. The thoughts, beliefs, and feelings that go along with each state of consciousness are quite different. To check in, notice if your thoughts and beliefs make you feel separate, inadequate, fearful, defensive, hopeless, powerless, critical, judgmental, confused, or alone. If they do, you can be sure these are created by and feeding your ego. Unfortunately, many of us experience these states of being a good portion of the time, and they don't make for a happy life. But you don't have to experience them. You can call these ego-based beliefs out into the light of compassion and shatter their hold on you by choosing more soul-centered ones.

Beliefs that make you feel connected, peaceful, openhearted, content, unselfish, nonattached to outcome, and generally at ease with life and all that it brings are created by and feed the soul. They are the ones you should nurture. Be ever watchful for the sneaky ego that constantly tries to take back thought control when you aren't looking and gently reinstate the soul as the director of your consciousness.

CHAPTER FOUR

WILLINGNESS

Many people have good intentions for change and yet languish for years in the tragedy of complacency, until eventually, tormented with sadness, sickness, or some other form of suffering, they are forced to change. In previous chapters, we have been getting ready for change, building an awareness of what needs to shift and the direction we want to go in. But even when we know what we *want* to do, we may resist action, because we are unwilling to live through the challenging process of change. We haven't developed the necessary willpower to do so. For this reason, it is helpful to honestly evaluate how *willing* you are to do your personal work. Only then can you take the deeper dive into developing the power of your will.

The expression "He lost the will to live" is telling, because will is the force that directs energy and creation. If we lose our will, we lose our energy, and without energy we have no life. The greater the will, the greater the flow of energy we have to create with. The less will force we have, the less creative power flows through us. The key to increasing our willpower is to become *willing*, which means that we overcome resistance to change and enter an easeful state of flow, riding the currents of life with a cheerful, cooperative attitude, even when things get rough.

Wisdom and will are the two principle powers governing our experiences in life. Wisdom is the knowledge of truth, our internal range finder. Will is the energy of the arrow we send forth, directing wisdom to its target manifestation. Without wisdom, will becomes simply a function of habit. And without will, even soul wisdom is impotent. For this reason, both are essential for maintaining health and vitality.

When wisdom and will are used optimally together, our choices don't come from what we think we *should* do, but from what we know we *must* do. As we step out of our comfort zone onto the edge of growth, we gain self-confidence. Yes, fear will arise at times, but with intuitive attunement, we can perceive whether fear is an indicator of actual danger or just an imagined threat to our psychological status quo. Finally, when we infuse our will with love, harnessing it to worthwhile activities with consistent effort, universal forces conspire to assist us in beautiful and unexpected ways.

The following practical tips for improving willpower will get you going in the right direction:

- Start small but undertake something challenging every day.

- Choose good company that is aligned with your goals and values. Stay away from unmotivated people.

- Be willing to withstand critical opinions of others.

- Become challenge-embracing rather than challenge-resistant.

- Affirm your power to resist bad habits.

- Practice strong concentration because where attention goes, energy flows.

- Limit desires for needless possessions.

- Eliminate doubt, which paralyzes will.

- Control emotionalism.

- Take time to be alone and practice introspection daily.

- Never give up on a worthy goal.

- Be on fire with purpose.

Am I willing to do the personal work I need to do?

Wishing our problems would go away, intending to do something, or even really wanting to change is not enough. All change requires some sacrifice, releasing old behaviors and beliefs, to make room for the new. This takes clarity and conviction. And *action*. You have to act with precision and consistency and keep acting until your desired change is firmly in place. It is your will that matters. How willing are you to choose the necessary action, again and again?

Because habitual response is always lurking, ready to drive your evolution backward, it is essential to centralize your attention on the highest soul qualities at all times. Willpower is a soul quality, part of your innate divine nature. The more divinely centered you are, the more powerful you become, because Spirit's unlimited power is ready and willing to support your will when it is rightly aligned. Concentrate and feel the force of your spiritual focus burning out all deficiency from the mind. Accept no thought that is contrary to your unlimited potential. Rise above the collective consciousness of limitation and choose freedom. Continuous calm use of the will shall indeed bring a response from the Infinite.

What is the weak link in my consciousness?

Fear, negativity, worry, doubt, laziness, belief in limitation, overstimulation of the senses, selfish motives, and even moodiness weaken the will. Inconsistency and the seeking of external validation paralyze it completely. If you are tired of being stuck, and truly know that you are ready and willing to try something new, then get curious about what lives in the shadow of your consciousness. Question yourself compassionately to expose your mistakes and shortcomings, but don't stop there. Try a new response in the face of an old pattern of reaction, emotion, or belief. Identify the saboteurs that work against your valiant efforts to change.

When you overcome the weaknesses that block your will-power, then life can once again move freely through you. Wonder is the miracle of newness, innate in us all as children. Look at things from a fresh point of view. Wonder about new possibility. Reclaim your innocence and let wonder replace anything in your consciousness that is impeding the willing flow of life.

What is this person or situation reflecting to me?

Our environments and the people in them are mirrors for our self-development. Like a 360-degree view that helps us see our blind spots, the things and people we are attracted to and repulsed by can tell us much about ourselves. Notice the specific traits that bother you in others, and how they may exist within you in some way. Then do the same for the positive qualities you admire in people, recognizing that you cannot see in another what does not also live within you.

As much as you might like to disassociate from the circumstances and people you believe are unlike you or undesirable in some way, if you truly seek self-awareness, you cannot. Everything that you perceive in another, positive and negative, exists within you, too. If you are willing to reflect on how that which is happening around you is a reflection and a result of what is happening within you, profound new self-awareness will come. As you develop the willingness to observe with less judgment and more inquisitiveness, you can inquire how the quality, behavior, prejudice, and so on that you see in the other is also a part of you. Then you can make any needed internal changes and also respond more compassionately to the other person.

In what way do I need
to ask for help?

The willingness to ask for help is, for some, the biggest hurdle of all. To them it implies weakness or incompetence. If this is how you feel, try allowing yourself to be the imperfect human that you are. Human beings are not islands or robots, capable of thriving in complete isolation or autonomy. We need one another. And we need to be needed. By not asking for help, you are blocking the flow, not just for yourself but for others, too.

Consider asking for help to actually be a sign of strength. By making clear and specific requests for help, we are taking ownership of our solutions in a different way. People are generally happy to assist if they are given specific, actionable ways to do so. And our willingness to engage their support helps them as well, because we inadvertently give them permission to ask the same of us when they need it. Although you may be asking for help today, tomorrow you may be asked to aid another. This exchange creates a flow of energy for us all. Tune in to your deepest needs. Assume accountability for them by asking for support in the ways that would be meaningful to you. Notice if this feels difficult and why.

How can I help others to help me?

Read this question again. It might seem confusing to think that you need to help others to help you. But at a closer look, you may notice that you block the flow of receiving more often than you are aware. Often, we resist assistance because of pride, or a fear of being perceived as weak, needy, or incapable. Imagine that you have asked for support on something, but then because you are still feeling resistant to the help, you negate the other person's gesture of goodwill by telling them how guilty you feel for accepting it, or how unnecessary their efforts were on your behalf. This behavior does not enable you to benefit from their kindness or aid.

Get out of the way. Stop doing, managing, and controlling and just be gracious. Practice gratitude and express appreciation. You may not always receive support in the exact way you want it, but if generosity is flowing toward you in any way, shape, or form, it is time to open to a new possibility of receiving. Continue reflecting on your state of willingness to identify any other ways you might negate help.

What obstacle to change am I ready to release today?

Consider what has consistently hindered you in the past. Notice any feelings that arise and how these feelings rule your decisions. Then, stop asking *why* life gave you this challenge. Take the obstacles in front of you and make them into stepping stones. Act with great will to interrupt the negative feelings and employ imagination to replace them with a new vision. Hold that long enough to generate a new feeling. By becoming truly willing to let go of any beliefs or behaviors that stand in your way of peace and freedom, your right course of action will become clear and you will begin creating a new reality.

Write an affirmation of your intention to move beyond that old hindrance now. Choose a joyful and optimistic approach to the day, even if outer circumstances are not exactly as you would have them be yet. Don't get discouraged if this inner obstacle tries to assert itself again. Be steady and determined in your willingness to move forward. The past cannot have a hold on you unless you let it. By owning your problems and looking at them as opportunities, you will find the positive approach to courageously overcome them.

What do I need to act on today?

The moment you move in the direction of needed change, you invoke the power of your will and invite the energy of the Universe to support you. Call yourself into action now by taking an outward step toward something that you have determined needs shifting. Think, "I could at least do . . ." Get curious and let your curiosity lead you who knows where. Open up any little possibility.

Your evolution is based on the million tiny choices you make every day. If you are feeling stuck, make a list of ten things, no matter how crazy, that you *could* do. You don't have to do all of them, but making the list will get the creative mind going. And there is always at least one small movement you can make in the direction of your dreams. This sends a clear, energetic message to life that you are serious about making change happen. Spiritual strength builds by setting realistic goals and taking consistent baby steps toward them.

Am I willing to have what I say I want?

As we attempt to change stagnant areas of our lives, we may notice that *we* are actually the problem, keeping ourselves from the very things we say we want. Strange as it may seem, we often work against our own wishes through the unwillingness to *have* what we say we desire in life. For example, let's say you are seeking more meaningful friendships. But you know that to have this would require you to extend yourself in new ways, and you have been hesitant to compromise your personal time and space. Because of this, you are not attracting new connections.

To answer this question requires some honest and perceptive self-analysis. Consider the things you wish for. Notice what you might be doing or thinking that could be keeping you from manifesting these desires. Analyze what this tells you about yourself at this time and if it indicates a misalignment with your chosen values. Think of how you could practice greater willingness, even if you don't have a clear sense of the actions you need to take.

What is being asked of me in this situation?

Sometimes the answer to this question is an obvious external action. But often it is not so simple. In many situations, it might be a more subtle, internal shift in relationship to what is happening. Obviously, we cannot control everything that happens around us, but we can change how we stand in response to it. Maybe we need to be more accepting, or maybe we need to set better boundaries. By undertaking conscious, willing change, we decide for ourselves why a particular challenge has come, what we can learn through it, or what we need to do. In this way, every challenge helps us build strength, resiliency, and faith.

Take a current situation in your life. Contemplate what you feel might be the reason for it being part of your experience at this time, and what is being asked of you in relation to it. Remember to practice great willingness as you decide the best way to behave and the right attitude to cultivate. Notice how your ego might try to block these choices in some way. Using willpower to choose well leads to freedom and as you invite more beauty and grace into your responses to life, you step into a harmonious flow with all that is happening.

CHAPTER FIVE

LESSONS

lthough the question, "Why?" often arises in our minds, as in "Why did this happen? Why me? Why now?" it is only helpful if we truly seek the lesson embedded in the occurrence. Otherwise "why-ing" is a waste of time and mental energy that would be better spent on questions that can lead us to solutions and peace.

If personal evolution is our goal, we must recognize that what happens to us does not matter as much as what we become through it. Struggling with resistance, self-pity, or blame just paralyzes our will and drains us, making us unable to respond effectively. Our strongest position is to see everything that arises coming specifically to benefit our spiritual growth. In this way, we learn to accept life on its terms and we conserve energy to learn what we need to move forward. As Brené Brown says, "Own the story and you get to write the ending. Deny it and it owns you."

A great way to reframe the typical, victim-tainted version of "Why?" is with one of the following questions: "What now?" "What am I to learn from this?" Or "What is the best response I can offer here now?" By shifting our whys to whats, particularly when things feel rotten and unfair, we make meaning out of challenges and move toward self-actualization.

When we embrace this paradigm shift of seeing every experience, positive or negative, as a spiritual lesson and a vehicle for our growth and learning, life starts to look radically different. We see daily trials through the lens of our soul's overall journey. Long-term gain replaces short-term ease. We use every challenge to fortify our willpower, every setback to practice endurance, and every failure as introspective information to help us activate greater success in the future. Problems become the necessary stimulant for our will, so we can remove any obstacles blocking the flow of our wisdom, power, and love.

Thoughts create our experience of reality, so what is most important is the viewpoint we hold on to about life. By reprogramming our minds to accept difficult situations in the right spirit, as our teachers rather than our oppressors, we build strength. As we develop a positive inner dialogue, judgment and negative self-talk no longer weaken us. We cultivate both curiosity and compassion and get out of self-pity into right action.

Through our willingness to learn, any trials that come serve to awaken us to our beautiful soul nature. We make space for light and love to flow through us unimpeded and open new doorways to our personal evolution.

What is life asking me to learn right now?

Think of life as a school, full of great teachers and unlimited information. There are probably subjects that you are getting high marks in and others you are failing. There are team-building exercises, word problems, presentations, personal essays, equations, multiple-choice problems, construction projects, and time-management assignments. Through these, hopefully, you are developing knowledge and experience but also the spiritual qualities of endurance, self-control, nonattachment, morality, and calmness. In order to graduate into the remembrance of your unlimited divine nature, you must pass all the tests in earth school.

If there is a subject that continues to give you difficulty, life is asking you to dig deeper in your studies. If you constantly feel challenged in the same ways, you have not yet passed that curriculum. Listen deeper for the necessary message. Change your approach to the solution. Get a personal tutor, coach, or mentor to help you gain more skills. Drop any defensiveness and be willing to see a new way. And don't worry. Through one lesson at a time, eventually, we all get the spiritual PhD.

What is my growing edge?

Fearless self-analysis is required for full personal develop-ment. Don't expect to avoid conflict or challenge. These are part of the game. Like stretching a muscle requires you to go to the edge of your current flexibility, stretching the inner self requires that you push the ego continuously but compas-sionately out of the way and cultivate greater soul qualities in its place. Avoid self-judgment, which serves only to delay your progress. Simply act to change that which you know needs changing. For instance, if you recognize a tendency toward impatience and angry reactivity, focus on all the ways you can practice patience and even-mindedness. Or if fear is in the forefront, study and practice courage.

Psychosynthesis, or personal integration, comes in four stages: knowing one's personality, taking responsibility for the elements of it that need changing, realizing one's true Self, and reconstructing the personality from the new center of soul awareness. Day by day, as you recognize the misalignments between the ego and the true Self, you can act to correct them. Your growing edge is the beautiful place where you bring your ego into the service of your soul.

What part of my spirit do I need to call back?

Most of us have a certain amount of energy residing in the past—in memory, regret, or reminiscence. If we have not forgiven someone, including ourselves, or we feel like we just can't move forward, we have blocked energy, and this prevents us from being fully present in the here and now. Sometimes, we may have given a part of ourselves away knowingly, and sometimes it happens unknowingly during a loss or traumatic experience, and this can prevent us from healing and evolving.

Take a moment and notice if a part of you feels missing in some way. If you have acted against your authentic self, or are letting a part of your spirit remain in the past, remedy that now by calling yourself back into integration. If you have not spoken or lived your full truth, articulate it today and embrace the things that matter to you, honoring your self-defined purpose for being. Drop regret and resentment and recognize that everything you are going through is exactly what is needed for your spiritual evolution at this point in life. Thankfully, at the soul level, we are always whole. By calling your spirit back from the illusions of fear, judgment, or self-negation, you will experience a sense of wholeness in your human life as well. To call your spirit back is simply to choose integration now. Forgive and move forward.

What good advice have I gotten that I haven't taken yet?

Our souls recognize truth when we hear it, which is why certain messages resonate for us. When friends and family offer caring words in our best interest or social media posts inspire us, we know we should take some of the good advice. But with the information overload most of us suffer from, it's easy for these positive directives to bounce off quickly, without taking actual effect. As we know, humans resist change, even if it is good for them. Implementation is the challenge.

As you ponder the best advice you've been given but haven't lived into yet, imagine your life five years from now if you don't act upon this counsel. Consider what has become of others you've known who haven't lived into this same wisdom, what the consequences have been for them. Really try to feel the outcome of potential nonaction. If resistance still remains high, look back at the questions in the last chapter on willingness and see where the block to change exists.

QUESTION 41

What can I learn from the most challenging person in my life?

This is similar to Question 30, in which you analyzed both the positive and negative traits that you perceive in others as a reflection of what might exist within you. Going a level deeper now, this question assumes that everyone is your teacher. Everyone. And the ones you resist the most, the toughest teachers of all, are the ones through which you will gain the most wisdom. Don't ditch class. Pay attention and really see what there is to learn.

There are reasons why each person or relationship is here now in your life. If you continually experience certain attitudes or behaviors from others, this indicates something about what you are inviting, or allowing, that you need in order to grow. Experiences repeat until we complete the lesson in them. Once the lesson is learned, relationship dynamics change. Patterns surface in accordance with your current need for evolution. So, ask yourself some tough questions about the patterns of experience in your primary relationships with parents, friends, and lovers. If you are frustrated by these repetitive patterns, determine what you need to learn and what you need to do differently with them.

In what ways am I inflexible?

We typically think of flexibility in physical terms, but it is just as much a mental quality. To adapt to the constantly changing circumstances and environments in our lives, we need the ability to adjust our thinking from old situations to new ones, moving fluidly rather than remaining stuck in habitual responses or thought patterns. If we are rigid in our perspectives or beliefs, it creates a narrow comfort zone in which we confine our lives. When they are challenged we pull back, like a tight body resists stretching. Unfortunately, rigid things break. But flexible ones bend.

To expand beyond your current mental inflexibilities, start practicing acceptance. Catch judgment when it arises in your mind and rather than spin in it, switch into curious mode. Choose learning rather than judging in order to gain flexibility. Everyone is entitled to their own opinion, so practice seeing things from several different points of view. If you choose to value harmony over defending your position, you will learn to tolerate differences and uncertainty. Your buttons will get pushed less and you will be able to respond with greater equanimity to conflict or chaos. The more graciously flexible you become in every aspect of your life, the greater will be your experience of ease and well-being.

What meaning do I want to give this circumstance in my life?

The concept of free will is key to this question. Although we do not choose all of the experiences that come to us, we do choose how we respond and what meaning we assign to them. It is empowering to look at every challenge as holding some hidden blessing just for us. In extreme cases of trauma or loss this may seem impossible, but even when all seems lost and dark, the light is hiding behind the clouds waiting for us to seek it. Life is not here to serve our comfort. It is unfolding to facilitate our evolution, whether we like it or not. If we resist, we suffer more.

We can change any experience by looking at it differently. Challenges come to bring out the hidden strength within us. Much of how we grow stronger, wiser, and more creative depends on whether we seek the lesson or blessing within difficulty. Sometimes, we just need to make up a meaning for it, to give ourselves a focus for inner growth. This requires willingness and courage. Ask yourself how you might be wasting time bemoaning a current situation. Then choose meaning and move forward.

What have I learned by utilizing my inner strength?

Think of a recent challenge you faced and what it taught you about your resiliency or ability to overcome. Like the weights on a machine at the gym, stressful times create the resistance we need to develop mental and emotional strength. As we engage our inner warrior, we learn that life requires both relentless optimism and unending willingness. It asks that we develop tolerance for the unknown and for temporary setbacks. It nudges us to ask for help, gently sometimes and with a firm kick at other times.

Maybe you have become more empathetic as a result of your own pain or suffering. Maybe you have learned how to keep a big-picture perspective and see how the stressful moment is happening within a much larger context of life. Hopefully you have learned how to rest and how to laugh at yourself as you fumble through. Give yourself lots of credit for the areas of growth you perceive and for the creativity you have embodied when you moved out of the problem and into the solution. We have all survived some challenge in life, and it's essential to give ourselves credit for the many ways we have thrived so far. Then we can draw upon these strengths and strategies when the next challenging moment arises.

Am I asking myself the right question right now?

If you want to get to New York, it is not helpful to ask how to make cheesecake. First, you need to determine where you want to go, internally or externally. It may be toward some kind of self-improvement or toward a physical goal. Then you need to metaphorically walk all the way around it, 360 degrees, looking at the journey from different perspectives. In this way, you will see the best route to get yourself there. The more possibilities you can formulate, the better. Brainstorm creative ideas to help you accomplish your goal.

Write down all the questions you can come up with. Inquire inwardly, several times, whether there are more. Then practice a period of stillness or meditation, clearing the mind of all analysis by focusing on the breath moving in and out of the belly. When your attention is completely absorbed in the sensation and rhythm of the breath, pause in the stillness and ask what question you most need to focus on right now. Trust your intuitive inner response. The right question asked at the right time can be life-changing.

CHAPTER SIX

ACCOUNTABILITY

Every mental or physical action we take, consciously or unconsciously, has an effect on our lives. Even inaction bears consequences. All of our future experiences will be affected by our present choices, actions, and thoughts, just as our present experiences are due to choices, actions, and thoughts made in the past. We are the architects of our future, right now, and we can decide to create consciously or sleepwalk into it. Through the simple use of our will, to do something or not, we create effects that bear fruit throughout time. In this way, we actively create our destiny in every moment.

Knowing this calls us to recognize the spiritual principle of accountability, which is embedded in the law of karma. Also known as the law of causation, or cause and effect, the word *karma* comes from the Sanskrit *kri* meaning "to do."

This energetic law, which includes the principle of free will, offers a reasonable way to understand life's seeming inequities. In essence, it is the only way to justify the discrepancies and injustices that are seen in human experience.

Under the law of karma, the effects of a person's actions, in this and previous lifetimes, follow them from incarnation to incarnation. Whether we like this concept or not, all of the illness, poverty, and disadvantage that we suffer are due to a transgression of divine law in this or a past life. If there were only one life to be had, it would be impossible to reconcile the imbalances of human experience with divine justice.

This kind of radical accountability may feel harsh at times because we cannot always see the correlations between cause and effect, but it becomes the ultimate journey of joy when we take responsibility and awaken from believing we are out of control into knowing that we are fully empowered. Through the beneficial law of free will, we have the power to change the course of our experience in the future. Whether we are aware of the original cause or not, we take responsibility for changing the effects of whatever has been done, by making responsible, conscious choices toward greater good now. Through the paradigm shift of accepting our circumstances, as products of our own choices and actions taken in the near or distant past, we become accountable to change. We release blame and choose freedom and strength instead.

Think of karma as a law of spiritual evolution. It is not an excuse to blame or judge someone for their difficult circumstances. Rather, it offers us an opportunity to step into the embodiment of greater soul qualities, such as selflessness, kindness, empathy, and compassion.

Adversity is the catalyst that makes us look beyond the day-to-day struggle toward our deep unlimited power.

We actually pull to us the experiences we need in order to evolve. And we repeat the lessons until, through self-examination, we discover the root cause of the disturbances and accept responsibility for changing. We punish or reward ourselves along the way through the use or misuse of our reason and will.

This is why values matter. Living from our highest values keeps us choosing righteously, unselfishly, and enables us to create good karma. In the game of life, selfishness takes us further from our true nature, setting us back an evolutionary notch, but selflessness moves us forward. As we come into a relationship of full accountability with ourselves and our life experiences, we find ourselves asking new questions, ones that lead to inspired new answers.

In what way am I keeping myself imprisoned?

Karma is not just created by action but also by thought. Negative thoughts, destructive judgments, anger, selfishness—these create our prison. Thankfully, we can liberate ourselves from these bad mental habits because we created them in the first place.

You are not bound by your karma. You have the free will to overcome it now and the capacity to accomplish anything if you learn to accept full responsibility. When you do this, you focus your energy into concentrated willpower that flows through you for material and spiritual success. Get clear on how you empower yourself and the ways in which you self-sabotage. Question your beliefs and don't let self-doubt put the brakes on your progress and evolution. Know that the choice is always yours and set yourself free today.

What am I not telling the complete truth about?

Radical accountability must be accompanied by radical honesty. Being honest with ourselves is often the hardest first step, but until we can do this we will not fully trust ourselves. We must look clearly at the motives behind our choices and how authentically we are living, or not. Our progress depends on ultimate integrity. All the ancient scriptures advocate right thought, right action, and right speech in order to become congruent with our highest Self. As we live completely in truth, our thoughts, words, and actions gain the power to manifest. What a tremendous gift and incredible responsibility this is. Notice any fear that rises around this.

List the reasons you may not be sharing or living your full truth right now. Then take a moment to feel how freeing it would be to do so. Create a personal pledge to step into greater authenticity. Follow through from idea to action, walk your talk, and keep your promises. Notice the increase in joy you feel as you do.

What would I do differently if I knew I was responsible for everything occurring in my life?

Karma is a great transformer if we have the eyes to see the opportunities before us. There are no accidents, and trials are born of our own making, for our own benefit, to help us evolve and to encourage us to make choices that bring true happiness. Ten people may share the same experience, but their reaction to it will vary in ten different ways. Attitude, and how we approach the tests life brings, matters. In practicing accountability, we lay aside the paradigm of victim or victor. We accept that we attract the circumstances we most need to learn from in this lifetime and responsibility for our own evolutionary progress. Accountability equals personal power.

As you introspect about what is currently happening in your life, affirm that unlimited power lies within you to change. By accepting full accountability for who and how you are, you will also see how you can choose a new way of being or responding to what is in front of you. Empowering yourself in this way, you will find freedom and peace.

Who or what am I blaming rather than taking responsibility?

If we accept that every aspect of life is, at its foundation, our teacher, then we can continue our inquiry into what we need to learn. Consider that all the people and events of your life are there because you have drawn them there in some way. Pay attention to the people and occurrences life has placed before you. They contain the lessons you must learn. What you choose to do with them is up to you.

It is futile to blame circumstances for what you are. As long as you are blaming anyone else for your state of being, you are denying your power. Think of a difficult situation in your life. Consider where you might be assigning blame rather than taking responsibility. Even if something has been done *to* you, you hold the key to freedom through how you choose to respond to the circumstance. Notice how your ego might be blocking your ability to move forward. Then spiritualize your thinking and use what karma has delivered to improve yourself. Take a giant step into radical accountability for all of your choices and reactions. Let any dissatisfaction you feel be motivation to change. Then get up and create yourself as you want to be.

How do I need to be
more courageous?

The word *courage* comes from the French word *coeur* meaning "heart." Think of courage as your heartfelt engagement with life. If this is lacking, you might feel unmotivated and low in energy. If courage runs strong then you probably feel passionate and excited about life. Take a few moments to be still and listen to your heart. Is it fully engaged with what occupies your time? Is your heart longing for anything? Sit with what arises and listen to the messages of your heart.

Then come up with one small action, some courageous step you could take now to honor your heart's longing. Even if fear is present, stay at the edge of your comfort zone, heart open and unwilling to let fear stop you. Imagine yourself five years into the future having made this courageous leap. Your future self is so grateful that you had the strength to move into positive action. Feel the pride and joy. Feel what a richer and more authentic experience of life has unfolded as a result of your courage and heartfelt engagement with new possibilities.

What is the best attitude to take or choice to make given this circumstance I am now experiencing?

By practicing simple mindfulness, we learn to observe our mental and emotional fluctuations with objectivity. Witnessing ourselves, we can take control over the ego's tendency to react impulsively and often self-servingly, creating more karma. Give yourself a few moments of mindfulness now. Practice observing detachedly what is present within you— thoughts, feelings, sensations. Just watch without following any of them. The more you maintain self-control rather than move into reactivity, the more connected you will become with your intuitive wisdom. Then, with your soul's direction guiding you, respond to what confronts you in a way that reflects your highest values and your innate divinity.

What change am I hoping for in someone else that I could more fully embody myself?

Most of us spend an inordinate amount of time thinking about how we want *other* people to change. We spend even more time arguing, pressuring, and manipulating them to change. And we waste a lot of energy being frustrated that at the end of the day those *other* people are just not changing in the ways we desire.

Consider the ways in which you would like the people in your life to change. Write these down. Then reflect on how *you* might need to change in the very ways you think someone else should. The fact is, you can never change someone else, so why waste your precious life trying? Focus on what you can do and lead through your positive example. Only others can elect change for themselves, but the incredible thing is that as you shift, they feel the effect and often make positive changes as a result. No guarantees, of course. They may never make the changes you want them to make, and you might have to adjust in relation to this. But regardless of what others do, you create greater internal well-being for yourself by being accountable for your *own* changes.

What is a fresh approach that could change my life today?

If you find yourself experiencing the same frustrations over and over, you may need to tackle long-standing problems from a fresh point of view in order to get new results. Try this exercise to help you shift perspectives. Tell the story of your life in the third person (he/she). Write the highlights from the standpoint of it all being perfect for his/her growth and highest learning, like a hero's/heroine's journey leading to a treasured goal. Feel the difference in telling your story from this joyful perspective instead of the worn-out perspective of personal struggle and suffering. Notice what approaches to change worked for your protagonist in the past and how you might apply them today.

All of the power of success lies in a strong yet flexible mind and a firm resolve. Get creative and think outside the box. Wholeheartedly reject any belief in deficiency or limitation. Concentrate on the beautiful, positive qualities of your soul and invite a totally new approach to something in your life to arise. Embrace possibility with a joyful, curious spirit and see where it leads.

Assuming karma is real, what would I like to complete?

Think of life like an ongoing karma project. You have come to learn at least one big lesson and to answer at least one core question, as well as many smaller ones. The main lesson and question are observable through the repetitive patterns of experience you have had, such as multiple betrayals, chronic money or health issues, or difficulty in love. Get clear on your assignment by considering the challenges you continuously run up against. Write down the essence of your test.

It is possible that you have worked for many lifetimes on this lesson or question, but because your soul wants to be free, you keep recreating it in new ways in order to overcome it once and for all. All the conditions that confront you now represent the perfect opportunity for you to complete this mission. You have within you the intelligence to understand and the power to overcome. Take a quiet moment in meditation to ascertain what needs completing. Then determine what you need to change in relation to those old patterns in order to finish your lesson or answer your question.

CHAPTER SEVEN

ACCEPTANCE

If we are unhappy, it's always for the same reason: we want something to be different than it is. Our happiness level correlates directly to the quantity and quality of things we want to be different at any given time. Sadly, we will remain forever discontented as life continues to deliver less than what we want, unless we change our basis for our happiness.

First, we can lose the expectation that life will go the way *we* think it "should." Instead we *should* expect curveballs, disappointments, and temporary failures. Rather than be pessimistic and resent them, we can see they are meant to stimulate us to reach greater heights.

To create the fertile soil for our continued spiritual progress, the key is practicing acceptance. Hand in hand with accountability, acceptance helps us focus less on the things happening *to* us, and more on what we are becoming *through* them. Everything becomes fodder for our soul's growth, and we create within us more lasting happiness and stability.

It is, in fact, possible to be happy even when challenges are occurring. This doesn't mean that we are thrilled by difficulty. It just means that as we practice accepting what is in front of us, we can move mindfully through any obstacles trying to block our strength and wisdom. Acceptance is a choice through which we regain control, but it takes effort and commitment.

Sometimes this means accepting that we can't change a certain situation, so we stop trying to do so. Or it could mean that we recognize a lesson we need to learn or an action we need to take. Regardless, acceptance is accomplished when we rise to a higher-level perspective in order to solve the difficulties that confront us. When we acknowledge our biases and resistance and show up to what is, with curiosity and compassion, then we make room for new perspectives to unfold. By letting go of how we think things *should* be, we enable new possibilities to arise.

Pain and suffering are reminders to awaken and seek deeper answers. By developing a richer understanding of what is actually happening rather than just going along with old stories and reaction patterns, we evolve. By practicing acceptance first, we can then access our spiritual power to create success. We step out of self-pity into positive action and accelerate our personal growth. Sorrow can only derail us if we adopt an attitude of defeat and give up the power of the soul. When we learn to accept a challenge but not be defined by it, we build strength of character and find peace.

How would it feel to stop judging everything as good or bad and allow this moment to just be?

Try spending the next hour watching how often you place an opinion or judgment on something or someone, *including yourself*. Most of us do this constantly without even being aware of it. Then notice the many ways in which you want something to be different from how it is. A lot of energy is spent being resistant. Notice how much time and focus you drain away from this present moment by ruminating on the past and any regrets or resentments that linger.

Then imagine letting all of that go; all of the judging, regretting, criticizing, and resisting. Clear the deck for a while and experience the moment as it is, without needing to form an opinion about it. When you fully allow things and people, *including yourself*, to be exactly as they are, you create a spaciousness in which to rest. Just practice being and enjoy the peace that comes as a result.

What would change if I let go of attachment and fear?

These common emotional states, attachment and fear, are indicators that we are in nonacceptance. Attachment usually arises because we fear what would be if that person, possession, or situation that we are attached to went away. We anticipate sorrow or feel agitated that our needs and desires might not be met in some way. In order to lessen the grip fear and attachment have on you, take a deep breath and relax your body. Soften around the feelings of worry and sink into a deeper level of trust and pure awareness.

Practicing nonattachment does not mean that we don't love. In fact, it means we open to an even greater state of love. Accepting people as they are leads us to empathy. Empathy leads us to compassion. Compassion leads us to great love. And this big love always feels better than the grasping of personal attachment or fear. To shift yourself toward this state of greater allowing, pray for release from attachments. Sing devotional songs to the Divine. Meditate and intentionally surrender to the Source of all love. These practices, done regularly, will liberate you and create space for a far more expansive love than you can imagine to arise.

When do I distract myself rather than being fully present with what is?

The tendency to move away from difficult feelings is natural, like withdrawing your hand from a hot object. But in the realm of mental and emotional health, you must learn to stay with discomfort long enough to give it voice and validation. Only then can you move beyond uncomfortable emotions to establish peace and balance. If you avoid or try to escape from your true feelings, then the pain festers beneath the surface of your life, influencing everything in unhealthy ways.

Take stock of the emotions that are present for you now, especially the unpleasant ones that you would rather suppress or deny. Place one hand on your belly and one hand on your chest. Take a few slow deep breaths and for just this moment, acknowledge any feelings like this: "I feel angry. I allow myself to feel angry. I accept that I feel angry. I make peace with feeling angry. I feel sad. I allow myself to feel sad. I accept that I feel sad. I make peace with feeling sad. I feel lonely. I allow myself to feel lonely. I accept that I feel lonely. I make peace with feeling lonely." Whenever you notice an impulse to move away from what is present, to distract yourself rather than stay with your feelings, pause and revisit this mindfulness practice.

In what way is my own attitude holding me back?

As much as we would like to blame bad circumstances, what we really have to deal with are our own bad attitudes. The mindset we bring to our relationships and circumstances makes a difference. If it is not optimistic, life-affirming, and kind, then it is holding us back and probably hurting others as well. If moodiness is habitual for you, reflect on why this occurs and what you need to do to counter it, so that it doesn't spread to those around you, causing more negativity or reactivity. Create a mood quarantine for yourself until you can choose thoughts and speech that propel you positively forward.

Bad attitudes are the ego's way of seeking to push our agenda forward. It may work temporarily, but ultimately it will backfire as people turn away, exhausted by your tendency to be difficult. Your outlook is a key factor in how you are perceived by others and how likely they are to want to connect with you. By cultivating an attitude of optimism and a joyful approach to life, you will magnetize more harmonious relationships and a host of new opportunities.

How can I make friends with uncertainty?

Most people get a bit out of sorts when things are uncertain in some way. Transition times in relationships or work can make us feel ungrounded and without direction. But if we learn to embrace times of uncertainty as opportunities to practice mindfulness, then we can remain attuned to our inner guidance for the next right steps. Dwell in possibility and don't limit life by confining it to your currently known parameters. Allow yourself to extend your imagination beyond your current comfort zones into the realm of the unknown or unproven, even if just the slightest bit. Visualize what you hope to manifest and keep that picture of the future solidly in view.

Use your resourcefulness to move toward this vision creatively and with a healthy dose of humor. When things don't go as expected, which of course they rarely do, practice nonreactivity and nonattachment. Keep reminding yourself that your soul has unlimited potential and is just waiting for you to expand into new possibility. Make friends with others taking similar risks to step beyond their fears into new horizons. As you do so with optimism, courage, and faith, you will find new capacities within you and a greater sense of ease with the unknown.

Who do I need to forgive?

A big part of our ability to move into full acceptance with life is determined by our ability to forgive people, circumstances, and even life itself for not delivering what we feel is fair. Clearly, no one gets everything they deserve or want, and we all make mistakes along the way. But we free ourselves from the self-made prison of resentment and regret when we choose forgiveness.

Forgiveness is really just another word for love—the love for self and life that we step into when we choose to live fully now, rather than constrict ourselves with bitterness or guilt. This is a completely inside job. Start electing love today by forgiving yourself for any way that you have allowed resentment or anger to affect your life. Forgive yourself for the shameful things you have done when you were in forgetfulness of your true essence as love. Then extend this same mercy to those in your life who have also forgotten or acted from anything other than loving intent. Feel the loosening of inner bondage that comes from this powerful form of acceptance. Regardless of whether anyone else changes, you secure your freedom and inner peace by forgiving.

Am I a facilitator of happiness and peace?

There are universal principles of harmony that through-out time, cultures, and philosophical systems continuously arise as the requisites for establishing a peaceful life. By living these principles, we ensure harmony within and without. If things get out of balance, you can return to these fundamental principles to determine what needs adjusting. They are closely aligned with the soul qualities we will assess in Question 100. They are as follows:

- Integrity
- Respect
- Responsibility
- Nonviolence
- Compassion

- Self-discipline
- Forgiveness
- Loyalty
- Humility
- Moderation

By embodying these principles, you stand in peace. Even if others do not do the same, you change your world. Do not dwell on negative thoughts or events, just offer love all around.

How can I practice acceptance through less doing and more being?

When there is a problem, it is natural to seek solutions, but if you move too quickly, you may miss the essential moment of simple acceptance that allows for the *right* solution to surface. You don't always have to know the answer immediately. Respect the dignity of your own, and others' learning process by not rushing to fix or push away the problem. Much healing can occur by offering your full presence and deep listening, to yourself and others, in moments of not knowing.

Start with a sixty-second reboot to take charge of reactivity and relax your body. With a few deep breaths, tense and release all of your muscles. Quiet the mind and cultivate the peaceful, centered strength that comes through the acceptance of your vulnerability. Call in the intention to be fully present. Be still and just breathe. Allow solutions to unfold naturally from your inner stillness.

When I meet people, do I focus on our similarities or differences?

Memories, expectations, and cultural biases color our experience of people unless we consciously release them. Notice your tendency to look for, or concentrate on, similarities or differences between yourself and those you meet. Rather than fear or resent that which is dissimilar, practice curiosity to learn new ways of seeing or doing things from those who have alternate customs, cultures, or beliefs. Instead of defending your paradigms and self-protecting by avoiding those who are different, practice compassionate acceptance and seek the connective tissue between you. Drop any judgmental comparisons; they kill joy.

Look for the connections that you can forge with people today, especially with those who seem the most different from you. Teach your children to do the same, making it a game to find all the things that are similar, and reinforcing the awareness that the same creative life force flows within us all. Regardless of skin color, political orientation, religion, or socioeconomic status, all humans share common experiences and emotions. By appreciating each person's uniqueness, you build the bridges of understanding and peace necessary in a world filled with conflict.

CHAPTER EIGHT

INSPIRATION

Our souls thrive on expression and flourish with creative manifestation. For this to happen though, we need to feed our inner spirit regularly with things that inspire and renew it. For some people this might be time in solitude or nature. For others it might be connecting with people of like mind in church or a meditation group. Some may draw spiritual nourishment from books or inspirational podcasts. It is good to have a variety of things that feel soul-nourishing, so there will always be one to reach for when we need an inspiration boost.

Additionally, we must watch out for the inner obstacles that try to block our path to inspired action. Restlessness is a big impediment. The prevailing habit that many people have of constantly checking their phones and social media is an indicator of scattered attention, and it impoverishes the soul. It is a futile attempt to assuage an internal emptiness with fleeting hits of pleasure. Such useless diversions distract us from going to a deeper place of reflection where we can draw inspiration from the field of potential.

The cure for this addiction to restlessness is immersion into the space and silence that connect us to our souls. For some, this is meditation, for others, contemplation or prayer. In any case, as we interiorize the mind, it becomes calm and focused. From the stillness, we draw forth inspiration that leads us to creative, purposeful pursuits.

Fear of or unwillingness to approach stillness are other hindrances to inspiration. These usually arise if we have unresolved inner conflicts or emotions. If this is the case, we first need to clarify our intention and then strengthen it with willpower and willingness as discussed in chapter 4.

When we step into the courage to be still and listen for the voice of inspiration within, we enable our best self to show up in life. We heighten creative flow by feeding the innate curiosity of the soul, offering it ever-expanding possibilities for expression. As we identify with our immortal, limitless essence, rather than the narrow ego self, we invite new accomplishment and true success. We move into inspired action by choosing activities and environments that support the development of noble soul qualities such as joy and courage. When we attune to love rather than fear, inspiration flows through us into manifestation and we experience change as renewal.

Where am I feeling flat right now?

Sometimes looking at what is *not* working helps us get to what will. Consider the areas in your life where you feel flat, bored, or stuck in routine. Notice how you may just be going through the motions or having the same conversations you have had too many times before. It is healthy to shake things up, like tilling a field to facilitate greater penetration of nutrients. Simple physical ways to change routines include drying yourself in a different rotation after a shower, using the opposite hand to brush your teeth, or taking a different route to work. New mental pathways can be established by refusing to have the same internal dialogues you have had with yourself, ad nauseam, in the past. Choose new thoughts. It's not easy, but it is possible.

Any way you can imagine to change up what feels stale or stagnant in your life is a great start. Make it a game to see how many things you can do differently in a day. Try a new hobby or different type of food. Have a fresh conversation. By loosening habituated patterns of action, you create space and availability for new inspiration to arise. Dishabituate yourself and soon you will be feeling free rather than flat.

What am I curious about?

Curiosity is one of our greatest guides to finding our next inspiration. It invigorates us by opening the door to new information and possibility. Allow glimmers of interest you hold about a subject, place, or activity to lead you into new worlds.

There is certainly something that you wonder about. Wonder is curiosity's counterpart because when you wonder, you become like a little child again, exploring and seeing the world through fresh eyes. No one ages well if they lose their sense of wonder. By being willing to learn and see things like a beginner or a child would, we stay young at heart and filled with inspiration. If this feels foreign to you, begin by thinking of five things you have always wanted to do but haven't yet. Then list five things you would consider trying that you've never tried before. Commit to exploring at least one of these new things this week.

What motivates me?

Motivation is what makes us want to get moving, to discover or accomplish something new. But sometimes we are motivated by unhealthy feelings like fear, lack, or shame. Trying to outrun these may get us moving, but it will never get us where we want to go. If we are hearing the words *I should* or *I have to* in our mind, fear is probably present, and if this is our only motivator, it will lead to resentment. Sooner or later, we will end up burning out or acting out in a way that shuts down our creative flow.

As explored in the previous question, curiosity is also a motivator. It is the soul's subtle pull toward things you may end up loving. And love, of course, is the strongest motivator of all. Love aligns you with conscious, grace-inspired action. Expand your love, and it will enable you to say no to the things that drain your energy and yes to the things that move you forward in a positive way. When your love, passion, and sense of purpose come together, you will be unstoppable. Simple yet profound is the choice between fear and love. If you seek inspiration, the choice must always be love.

Can I imagine a
different possibility?

Another powerful soul quality that kick-starts creativity and sparks inspiration is imagination. Every great invention, artwork, and scientific discovery began in someone's imagination, drawn from the infinite well of universal wisdom. Sadly, sometimes the rational mind tries to limit the imagination by judging it as impractical or intangible, but we must silence the inner critic if we want to expand in possibility. Imagination is the soul's call to the vast field of potential.

Consider a circumstance that you feel stuck in right now and allow yourself to imagine twenty possible ways to get unstuck. Don't limit your list by analyzing the feasibility of things. Remember, this is an exercise in imagination. Let yourself be as creatively free as possible. You can always edit later. Write down all twenty ideas, even if you really have to stretch yourself. You may never act on any of them, but just by doing this you will start to be more inspired. Imagine how acting on at least one or two of your ideas would feel. Then consider going for it.

SPARK CHANGE · 100

What will I fill my heart up with today?

Just as we need healthy food, water, rest, sunlight, and fresh air to fuel our physical bodies, we also need positive messages, spiritual inspiration, and encouragement to fuel our hearts. Begin by thinking about what you have been moved by recently—some picture, conversation, or message that touched your heart. These are indications of things you could reach for if you need refueling.

If something excites you or surprises you in a positive way, follow it. You can start with even the smallest flower or ray of light. Think of how many poems and paintings have sprung from an artist's careful noticing of simple, quotidian detail. Allow your heart to show you what inspires it by taking time to observe with more care and absorb with greater openness. Notice what qualities stir your soul: peace, compassion, humor? Seek out the people and environments that express these qualities. Make both large and small choices that fill your heart with joy.

What am I doing when
I feel the most alive?

Think of when you feel radiant, like you are shining from the inside out. You are full of energy and feel purposeful and meaningfully engaged. There is a pureness to this vibrancy that comes from just being you. The activities and creative pursuits that light this inner fire are what you are meant to be doing. These make you feel peaceful, and yet energized at the same time, ready to start each new day fresh.

If what you are doing does not give you these feelings, at least some of the time, it may be a sign you need to reevaluate what you are devoting time and energy to. Maybe you have chosen familiarity over full aliveness or have fallen into habitual ruts or the tendency to take the easy way. If it feels like it's time to light your inner fire again, identify at least one thing that makes you feel engaged and purposeful. Then expand it as much as you possibly can. Notice how your inspiration quota goes up as a result. This is positive self-challenge, when you walk intentionally toward the edge of the known and look beyond to what you might create.

What has renewed my inspiration in the past?

It would be impossible to stay inspired all day, every day. Like a pendulum, we swing in and out of inspiration, but it is important to know how to right ourselves when we have gotten out of balance. Look to the past to remember times when you have felt supercharged and assess what made you feel this way. Although the same things won't always have the same effect as you grow and evolve, everyone has activities that renew and refuel them. Maybe a change of scenery or a short trip helps you. Or just having quiet time alone to think. Self-care activities like massage, exercise, or reading can re-spark inspiration for many.

Maybe there is something that has been crying for your attention, but you have not stopped long enough to listen. Slow down and let yourself be bored enough to give creativity space to bloom. Imagine the things you would do if you didn't have to work or money didn't matter. Or try giving yourself a fun goal to work toward or a new incentive to keep life fresh. Finally, remember to just play.

How can I choose more freedom?

Freedom does not mean you quit your job or leave your spouse. To be free is to live life on your own terms. It means letting go of caring so much about other people's opinions and prioritizing your own needs to an equal degree as the needs of others. It means choosing to engage with the people, places, and things that allow your heart to sing. Spirit wants to express through each of us, but we must make the brave choice to be who we truly are. In this way, we open the channel for our own happiness and for the complete expression of the divine energy in manifestation.

If it is difficult to imagine how to do this, think of someone you know who does and let them be your role model. Notice the subtle ways you tend to shrink back rather than go big. Reflect on how much you are, or are not, living your own life.

If I gave myself permission to be fully who I am, what would I do differently?

We are all conditioned by our cultures and social circles, which affect how we speak and act. This is not a problem unless we are modifying ourselves in an inauthentic way. It is true that by stepping fully into our authenticity, we risk other people's judgment. But if we don't, then we have to live with our own internal disappointment. Go ahead and give yourself a minute to consider the worst possible scenario of being 100 percent *you*. So what if you try something and fail, at least you tried. We are all works in progress and any setback can become fuel for future forward momentum if we let it. Write down all the ways in which you have learned or grown through failures in the past and use this inspiration to keep stepping into the most authentic expression of yourself.

Give yourself *full* permission for just a moment to imagine what being you with no holding back would look like. Something in your heart wants fuller expression. Some aspect of your life wants to be more deeply felt. Knowing your answer to this question is so powerful because then you can gauge on a daily basis how much you are allowing fear to rule your life, or not. You can only fail if you quit. If you get up again and keep going, then you win. You win the prize of strength and conviction in being yourself.

CHAPTER NINE

KNOWING

To grow our lives into their greatest potential, we must remain both grounded in rational thinking and open to intuition. These two different states of awareness, when harmonized, guide us safely from our presently known places into exciting, uncharted territory. Rational thought enables us to weigh the pros and cons of potential decisions and conduct a thorough analysis of our current capacities and shortcomings. Intuition, the voice of the soul, attunes us to objective truth. It leads us beyond what our limited, sensory mind can perceive to the most joyful possible expression of our true Self.

Intuitive knowing is the highest form of intelligence because it is directly connected to Source wisdom. It boosts imagination, creativity, and confidence, and helps us get clear on our purpose and calling in life. Our relationships improve because we are empathetically tuned in to the feelings of others. Intuition enables us to identify and handle problems more efficiently and therefore reduces stress.

Most of the time we operate from the egoic, thinking state, but if we remain solely reliant on our own self-sufficiency, we will block the wisdom of intuition and miss essential information necessary for our evolutionary progress. Fortunately, we all have the power of intuition, just as we all have the power of thought. It just needs to be developed. A daily routine of silence is undeniably required so we can attune ourselves to this inner power of truth perception. First, we must quiet the thinking mind, which tries always to be in charge. This can be done through a simple form of meditation in which we rest our full attention on one thing at a time, such as the breath or a mantra, to build inward focus. As we withdraw the mind from its restless outer focus, we quiet the nervous system and calm the body. In the interiorized state, when we are open, receptive, and trusting, spiritual sensitivity awakens, and we achieve balance between reason and intuition.

When calmness and concentration are developed we hear the response of the soul that guides us away from doubt and fear to liberation. Surrendered into a tranquil, intuitive receptivity, we tap a higher level of consciousness and appreciate a serene and secure sense of joy. As we make friends with stillness, peace fills the depths of our being and we always know our right course of action. Humility, far more than an advanced intellect, makes this true wisdom achievable. The gentle voice of the soul reveals our unbroken connection to infinite truth.

As a child, was my intuition
encouraged or invalidated?

Many things are kept from children's sight, for their protection at times, but also because families often have contradictions between what they instruct and what they live. If there are hidden emotions or motives, children sense them but learn to doubt their perceptions of what is true if they are not acknowledged. If this was the case for you, begin to test your intuitive sense every day. Listen to the ways your body sends signals of truth or discrepancy. Learn to notice internal red flags, sensory signs that something is actually different from how it appears externally.

Pay attention to intuitive thoughts or gut feelings as they arise and keep a written log of how they play out. Over time, you will learn how your intuition communicates with you. For some people it is a visceral, physical feeling. For others, it could be a mental whispering of truth or a visual flash. Additionally, learn to heed your conscience as it is an important reinforcement to your intuition. Conscience nudges you toward authenticity. By listening to it, you will increase self-knowledge and be on your way to a more integrated life.

What is preventing me from being quiet inside?

In our overstimulated world, where constant connection is the norm, we have become unaccustomed to silence. It can feel scary at first. You may sense emotions you are hesitant to face or a need for change that you are not quite ready to deal with. Any fears that lurk in the shadows, the ones you keep at bay through busyness, threaten to come crashing into view. In order to befriend silence, you must first recognize what might be keeping you from it.

Look courageously at the ways you may not have been completely honest with yourself or another, or how you may have neglected your spirit or squandered your life energy. Breathe with whatever appears, just observing, not judging. Invite the discomfort or fear that you've been avoiding to join you in the quiet of self-reflection for a compassionate intervention. Over time, as you replace fear with self-compassion, you will no longer feel awkward or lonely in the stillness. The shadows of the mind will clear and greater intuitive awareness will arise. Silence will become the place in which you meet yourself fully and where you hear the consistent, calm voice of your soul speaking.

SPARK CHANGE · 110

What inner conflict is causing me disharmony?

Ongoing physical tension, growing impatience, conflicting emotions, moodiness, overwhelm, and anxiety are all signs of stress, which indicate a disharmony within your being. These often arise if there is a fundamental inner conflict or some incompatible personal commitments. This kind of suffering can be your teacher if you listen and learn from it, but if you ignore or deny its presence, or allow it to go on too long, it can become chronic mental and physical pain.

Consider the things you feel conflicted about, such as disliking your job but sensing it is where you must stay because of finances or wanting to pursue a creative dream but judging it as impossible. Name the discomfort, whether it is physical, mental, emotional, or spiritual. Write down all the words you can think of that relate to it. Just brain dump for a few moments. Then notice the correlations between the mental and the physical or between the emotional and the spiritual experience. For instance, if you are having digestive issues, you may have written down words that reflect the physical symptoms such as stuck, full, bloated, or irritated. You might then notice that you have been feeling emotionally stuck or mentally irritated. Play with the parallels between categories of experience until you can clearly see the root of the disharmony and what it needs for resolution.

How can I know the difference between fear and intuition?

Fear is, in some cases, an intuitive warning signal, alerting us to real danger in a situation or relationship. But fear can also be triggered by phobias and neuroses, sending the over-wrought psyche into a tailspin that is anything but intuitive. Fear is like a jackhammer in the subconscious that blocks inner awareness and almost always keeps us from hearing our deeper wisdom. If we were not afraid, we would know exactly what needs to be done and how to respond to what is happening.

There are some very consistent signals that differentiate irrational fear from true intuition. If you feel agitated, restless, or disquieted, or want to escape or react quickly, these are signs of fear. When you feel peaceful, consistent, and integrated in your mind and your heart, these are signs of being connected to intuition. In fear, you will rush in or out, but when you are intuitively guided, you wait patiently for the right timing and the surety of true knowing. You may still sense something negative or scary, but you feel calmer in relation to it and confident in your ability to handle what may come, even if it is challenging. Anchored in intuition, you assess the value of things based on whether they foster peace of mind and trust that whatever does is the right next step.

What is my intuition whispering to me now?

The voice of intuition is always sending subtle signals, nudges toward your highest good. These may sound like repetitive thoughts urging you toward change. Or they may come as physical sensations such as discomfort in the gut or a racing heart, when you start to move in the wrong direction. Regardless of the delivery, the messages from intuition remain consistent, patiently waiting for you to pay attention.

It is up to you to listen to the whisperings of your inner wisdom. Even if it doesn't make perfect sense outwardly or seems too difficult to implement at the moment, listen and trust. You will know that the guidance is right because it feels peaceful and steady. You will sense assurance and support, even if what your intuition is urging you toward is difficult to accomplish. It will always lead you in the right direction. Don't let fear block your brilliance. Fear can have no power over you unless you let it. You are a wise, free soul here to manifest greatness, and your soul knows what that means in this moment.

What do I know for sure?

To live a life of meaning and purpose takes vision. As you expand your understanding of yourself and the world around you, you form an image of your place within the whole. Intuition enables you to cultivate this personal vision. Think about the life you wish to embody and the self you wish to become. Take some time to consider what is going to be required to get from where you are now to this new version of life and self.

Clarify what you currently know *for sure*, as this will keep you on track. Determine what aspects of the old you that keep you trapped or disengaged need to be released. Know what you are willing to compromise, and what you are not. Be honest with yourself about how you could more completely live what you know inside is right. This is the practice of cleaning the inner window so your divine radiance can shine out through your life. Get clear about who you are and where you are headed and then move anything that blocks your inner light out of the way.

What can I learn by accepting that I "don't know"?

The mind loves to categorize and sort things in a comfortable, predictable way based on what it knows and has experienced. Because of this we make many assumptions based on the past, which may or may not be true in the present. We must let go of believing that we know everything in order to begin to know anything at all. Allowing ourselves to *not know* is an important part of the process of coming *to know*. Relieving the pressure of having to know the answer at any given time gives us the opportunity to explore a deeper awareness. True knowing arises from a natural state of being.

When you enter the flow of being, undoing all that you think you are, then intuitive knowing can arise. In pure awareness, you no longer need to posture for the preservation of the created self. There is simply a spacious, natural balance in which you drop into trust of the soul. Here the body becomes the instrument of the inner spirit, and your life becomes its expression. Clear out the need to know the answers now. See how much learning comes from allowing yourself *not to know* and how living in this open space feels free and light. Sometimes all that is required is to pause, wait, and listen longer. Trust the process.

What is true?

Beyond personal experience or preference, pure truth exists. The recognition of such objective truth is only available to us through soul perception within. This is why, when we hear a universal truth, it seems familiar, as if we already know it, because we do. How open and receptive we are to this inner realm of knowing determines how much other knowledge we can attain and how rapidly.

With little intuitive receptivity, you may be exposed to an experience or to information and yet not learn or comprehend anything. Intuition is the faculty that enables you to grasp quickly the meaning and purpose of a situation or a problem, as well as the ability to know the simplest solution. It is wisdom from the inner Source and is independent of outer knowledge, which is based on mental or sensory awareness. A regular practice of meditation is a wonderful way to liberate yourself from personal bias and attachment and tap the wisdom of the cosmos.

What do I need to know in this moment?

Create a quiet space for meditation. Gently close your eyes and breathe, relaxing a little more with each breath out. Focus your awareness on the body relaxing, every breath deepening your sense of letting go. Allow all thoughts to drift by like clouds floating in a distant sky, not holding on to anything. This is your moment to rest within and to access divine guidance. Affirm that you are now opening to your highest intuitive wisdom. Be still and trust.

Then ask, "What do I need to know in this moment?" Pause and listen. An answer may come quickly or you may just feel deeply peaceful in this moment, without the need for a response. Don't worry if nothing arises immediately; information may come later. Witness any thoughts, images, or sensations that surface without judging or analyzing them. If you have a specific, pressing decision to make, you can try asking for intuitive guidance using yes or no questions. Imagine that in one hand you are holding the word *yes*, and in the other hand you holding the word *no*. See the letters and feel their weight. After you ask a direct question, you might have the sense of being pulled toward yes with feelings of joy or relief. In contrast, a no response might involve a feeling of numbness or of being blocked or a sense of dread. The most important thing is to remain still and calm. Intuition speaks quietly and will easily be drowned out by the rational mind rushing in to analyze. For now, just practice stillness and deep inner listening.

CHAPTER TEN

LOVE

L ove is the harmonizing principle of the Universe. Unfortunately, we regularly get pulled *out* of harmony by the influences of the world, our desires, and our habits. To align ourselves with love requires the strong and intentional choice to be a loving person, not because of what has been given to us or what we hope to gain, but because it will create within us the greatest peace. By choosing love, we choose harmony, and as a result we gain the strength and clarity it takes to navigate life's chaos with a tranquil mind and an unbreakable heart.

All of the self-reflection that we have been doing helps us see what stands in our way and makes us ready to confront fear, doubt, and judgment when they arise. As we orient our lives and commit our hearts to love, we liberate tremendous power. Love enables us to be self-disciplined and resilient. It stimulates our will, giving us the incentive to change and to do the work of personal evolution. It keeps us from self-sabotage and leads us to the ways we need to rebalance.

Love is like our North Star, helping us to constantly self-correct, and a deeper commitment to loving is the antidote to any emotion or thought that may arise to throw us off course.

To follow the path of love takes just a simple choice: to prioritize love, no matter what. If we listen, love is constantly whispering its wisdom through our intuition. It gives us courage and faith to pursue the things that bring meaning to our lives, and the more we dwell in the energy of love, the more profound our experience of love will be in all of our human relationships.

As we follow the path of love, we aspire to be our best selves, to live intentionally, and to overcome anything that might draw us away from this state of being. We overcome fear and fall into a faith-filled love with the sacred Singularity in which we seek to serve the universal good and harmony of all beings. Amidst the sorrows of being human, this divinely focused love brings the ultimate fulfillment. When we taste the transcendent nectar of spiritual love, we commit to that which is greater than ourselves and accept this moment, and all that it holds, as an opportunity to offer more. Focusing on the good, the beautiful, and the true, we become free, fully embodied in our true nature, as love itself.

In what ways could I choose love more?

To act lovingly, especially when many around you may not be doing so, requires courage and trust in the supreme power of love itself. It is far too easy to close down in self-protection rather than risk being vulnerable. In the face of anger, fear, or despair, we justify defensiveness, yet really it is nothing more than our inability to rise to a greater measure of love. To choose love requires a willingness to risk, if nothing else, the exposure of our tender hearts. The good news is that in return, we gain immeasurable strength and peace.

Where love lives, peace and joy expand. Where it does not, friction, disharmony, and conflict reign. Choosing love means that you do not wait for circumstances to be ideal, or other people to act perfectly. It is an orientation to life, to all of your decisions, because it is what will free you from inner conflict and bring you lasting happiness. Notice whether your thoughts, words, and actions are taking you closer to or further away from love and decide definitively which direction you want to move in.

How do I need to heal my love story?

We have all been hurt, *not by love*, but by the manipulation or lack thereof. These transgressions occur when someone is separated from their true spiritual nature. Sadly, many people are and behave badly as a result. If you have been hurt in what you believed to be a loving relationship, or if you were made to think that you are unlovable in any way, it is time to rewrite your love story. Commit right now to your highest good and be done with anything or anyone that is toxic to your well-being. If unloving words were spoken to you in the past, check to be sure you are not repeating the same words to yourself internally. Monitor your thoughts and eliminate any that are negative or discouraging. Cherish yourself as much as you want others to cherish you and support yourself as you hope to be supported by others.

Any perception of worth, or lack thereof, is created by identification with the ego self, which by nature is always imperfect. However, at the soul level, the concept of worth doesn't exist. This higher aspect of Self *is* love. If you do not currently know yourself *as* love, it is time to get to know the real you. Your true Self *is* pure spiritual love. Do not allow anyone or anything to undermine your connection to the love that you are. Center your self-knowing, your very life, in this truth. Identify yourself completely as love, and you will be able to release any old pain attached to the ego. By choosing to live with your consciousness deeply anchored in the truth of your true nature, your new love story will be one of total freedom and joy.

Is my consciousness based in love or fear?

Our ego nature loves to be self-sufficient, trusting entirely in its own strength. But without the sustenance of Source, we eventually tap our personal capacity and are left feeling limited and afraid. Fear mutes the voice of the soul, closing off access to our intuition. Although it often happens, we need not wait until we hit the bottom of our personal ability tank before we open to the grace of love.

The recurring thoughts you allow to fill your mind determine your overall state of consciousness. If you notice that your mind is filled with worry thoughts, it is a sign that you are probably trusting too much in yourself and not enough in your loving Maker. To shift from fear to love, begin by acknowledging and accepting your vulnerabilities, thereby creating an opening for Source to work with you. As you live more from trust and love, decisions become easier and more peaceful. A consciousness based in love will never lead you astray.

How would I act in this experience if I were anchored in love?

Willingness opens the floodgates of possibility. Even if you don't know *how* to apply love in a particular situation, you can be willing to try. You may need to practice letting go of your personal agenda or desire. Or you may need to ask more questions in order to understand at a deeper level what is happening. At times, you might need to give some space to another person to show your love. You may also need to set boundaries, if someone is not being kind or respectful, in order to choose love for yourself.

Pay attention to when you feel inclined to close your heart. This happens when the ego takes over, and we feel limited in our capacity to love. In these moments, we must lean into our trust of Source love and draw from that universal, infinite well. Then we will be able to reopen our hearts and expand our current capacity to give, finding ever-new ways to connect with others. Notice how you typically show love and explore new ways to do so. Think of ways in which you have received another's kindness or compassion, how that affected you, and how you might do the same for someone else. Through every practice of loving, we evolve.

How could I be more thoughtful of those around me?

The decision to expand our love cannot stop with the people we feel closest to. With colleagues, family members, and strangers there is always someone to whom we could offer more compassion or care. Pausing to consider how someone else feels, what their needs are, is the first step toward thoughtful action. Consider who might benefit from your quality time or attention right now. This could be as simple as listening attentively while a family member vents about a challenge, doing a little more than your share for a colleague who is overwhelmed, or simply being patient with a stranger. A little thoughtfulness goes a long way in life.

By noticing what other people's needs are and how you might offer assistance, you are practicing thoughtfulness. At the same time, take care that you don't try to fix someone else's problems. When friends are mired in difficult emotions and distracted by pain, the important thing is for you to hold compassionate space for their suffering and share your vulnerabilities as well. Encourage them as they find their own solutions and remember together that challenges are part of the learning process. In this way, thoughtfulness becomes a circle of giving and receiving that benefits all.

How can I be of greatest service?

Selfless service, or *seva*, is a spiritual practice that benefits both the giver and the receiver, because what we offer to another in essence we are offering to ourselves. Look for ways to make a meaningful contribution by uniting what you love to do with the needs you perceive around you. Ask people how you can help, what support from you would look like to them. Ask them to tell you what they need and then watch for any unwillingness based in your ego that tries to hold you back from this service.

There are innumerable ways to serve, but as simple as it sounds, kindness is one of the greatest acts of service we can undertake. Much spiritual progress can be made by just being kind, and what a sweeter world it becomes when we serve one another with kindness. Whatever you say or do, say or do it with love. Love so completely that you forget to notice if you're being loved or served in return. The more you enter self-forgetfulness, the more you will experience bliss.

What sadness is keeping me separated from love?

Often when we are in doubt, sorrow, or turmoil, we abandon love, especially self-love. But the further we stray from it, the worse we feel, alone and adrift. This separation from love is the basis of all unhappiness and it is based in the egoic mind. Thankfully, we have only to reconnect to our souls and the love that waits within them to heal the false belief that we can ever be separate.

In your daily meditation, begin with an intention to connect to the love that is your life-sustaining energy. As you call your spirit back from the illusions of fear, loss, and resentment and concentrate on your divine essence, you breathe the energy of love into life again. With faithful attention and deep devotion to love itself, you will see through the delusion of separation and its resulting sadness. It is impossible to be separate from love, even for one moment, because it is the core of your very being.

What might be different if I replaced judgment with love?

Good, bad, right, wrong, want, don't want: our minds are constant judging machines. Track it for a day and you will see this tendency is pervasive and incessant. Sadly, it separates us from one another and from love.

The reality is, our problems are not over there, in the other, as much as they are in the lens we choose to see others through. Rather than assess what's wrong, choose to look for what is right. Instead of focusing on the differences between you and someone else, look for what you have in common. Rather than criticize another's weakness or incompetency, seek their strengths and praise their shining moments. When you accept people's inevitable imperfections, then you can ask new questions that will lead to new outcomes, such as understanding and empathy. By giving love and respect even to those you don't agree with, or to those who misunderstand you, you expand your capacity for compassion and in this mercy, you are set free.

In what form do I most want to know love?

Mother, father, friend, lover, guide, protector, advisor— you name it, love *is* it. We each feel the need for love in specific ways, usually based on what we have not gotten enough of. Because Source love is available in all of these forms and more, we can call in the type of love we most need by connecting to that aspect of divine energy. If you are ready for a different experience of love, an embodied knowing of it, try this experiment. For one full day, get out of your head and into your heart. Act only in love, in as many ways, big and small, as you can, particularly in the aspect of love you most want to know. Don't look for what you are getting in return and don't second-guess yourself. Just do the experiment, see what's different and how you feel.

When you call out to love with your whole heart and live into it with your whole being, it cannot help but come to you in the desired way. Be ready for miracles. This beautiful practice will expand your awareness of Spirit, and show you that love surrounds you in ever-new, ever-available, and ever-diverse forms.

CHAPTER ELEVEN

PURPOSE

Every single soul that embodies into human form has come for a purpose. The unique purpose we are here to express in this lifetime is what we must discover. Known as *dharma*, it is revealed through the pursuits that bring us joy, the passions that keep us up at night, and the ways in which we feel called to serve the greater good. When we are able to live "on purpose" we feel radiantly alive and inspired.

Because the soul is infinite in its spiritual nature, it also wants to express a myriad of things in human life. Compassionate self-inquiry helps clarify what will light the fire of the soul's passion at any given time. Every stage of life offers a new opportunity to identify what is important and what will fill our inner well. Our sense of purpose may shift many times, and it is up to us to keep assessing our reason for being here now.

To do this, we must keep the intuitive channel clear by replacing thoughts or beliefs that pull us away from love with ones that center us in it. The deepest calling of our hearts can only be heard when we quiet the outer forces that pull on us and dive deep into the wisdom of our inner spirit. Every day, we can remember to listen to the beautiful soul that lives within, so that it may reveal why we are here and for what we have come.

By maintaining a conscious conviction to live with purpose, we prioritize the soul over the ego. As a result, any sacrifices seem like small offerings for the reward of unshakeable spiritual strength and wisdom. Inner conflicts are resolved and hard decisions are made with ease because soul-driven values light our way. Although other people may not always understand or agree with our choices, we feel joyful, regardless of external validation. When we are aligned with our heart's calling, initiative flows. We make choices based on our highest values and develop real clarity of purpose, which leads to certain success and lasting happiness.

Creating purposeful activity that fosters ongoing personal evolution, rather than just passing time with superficial things, we remain vital, even into old age. And by living into our purpose, we are able to graciously help others find theirs as well. A purpose-driven life brings joy to everyone it touches.

What is my unique purpose at this moment in time?

The word *dharma* comes from the Sanskrit root word *dhri*, meaning "to uphold or support." In the grand sense of it, dharma is the law that upholds the divine order within creation, the principle of truth which, if we are aligned with it, establishes harmony in our lives and keeps us from suffering. To step into your personal dharma is to make the goal of your life conscious and to align individual purpose with service to the greater good of all beings. There is a way in which your special skills and passions can contribute to the well-being of others. When you determine what your dharma is, you feel at peace, connected in heart, mind, and soul.

Without comparing yourself to anyone else, listen to your heart and think about what you have to offer: a talent, skill, or resource you have that can help one person, or a million people, today.

This creative gift could be extremely simple or vastly complex. It yields satisfaction through engagement, not just results, and time flies when you are immersed in it. When you love what you are doing, you will do it for a long time without exhaustion or depletion. You actually get fueled by the doing and feel there is always more to share. Consider who needs what you have to give now or to whom you can give something that will matter. You will know you are on the right track when you feel yourself living the best version of you and your heart is open wide.

Why does my gift matter?

Once you have answered Question 91 about your unique purpose, imagine if you were to die without ever accomplishing it. Something would be absent in the world. Maybe many things. A critical link in the fabric of the whole would be gone. Others would miss out on what you had to share, and your soul would depart unfulfilled in its purpose this lifetime.

Imagine what people who knew about your talent, skill, or gift would say about *why* you didn't use it. Then consider what you would rather have them say and live into that! It isn't selfish to live purposefully. In fact, it is essential for the greatest good of all. Make a list of all the ways you would benefit others by sharing your unique gifts. Don't deprive the world of what you have to give. We are each an essential part of the singular reality, and as such, we are meant to contribute in some way.

If I could, what one thing would I change about the world?

We can sometimes feel small and powerless to make a difference in this big world, but every one of us has something to share. Reflect on what concerns you in the world today, what you deeply care about—a cause, an injustice, a shared human experience. Knowing what you would like to change is a great directional sign toward your purpose. Think of making even a small difference as your spiritual responsibility. Whether what you offer is the first drop in a big bucket toward change or the last one that makes the bucket brim over into transformation, your drop matters.

If you are not already participating in one or two meaningful ways of being such positive change, begin today. Step outside your comfort zone and claim your power. Whether you invest your energy locally, nationally, or globally, your contribution will be felt and appreciated by many. Any action taken with love is a great action.

Is this activity really what I need to be doing?

Like the accumulation of material goods, we also accumulate activities, some of which are purposeful, many of which are not. Eliminating those that do not serve our highest values or do not give meaning to our lives or the lives of others is an important part of developing clarity of purpose. Like clearing our closets of unused items taking up unnecessary space, clearing our days of activities that have little meaning frees space in our minds and hearts for things that mean more.

The first thing that came to your mind when you read the question is what you should start reflecting upon. But don't stop there. Go through all of your daily activities and assess whether they are *really* what you need to be doing and if they contribute to you feeling purposeful or not. See if what you give the most time and energy to on a regular basis is serving your personal evolution. If not, reevaluate. Consider how your energy could be best utilized, because not fully using your talents does not serve you or anyone else. Let yourself fully shine.

What continually pulls me forward in life?

Think of the things that make you want to get up in the morning. When you are involved in these activities, creations, or pursuits, you feel wholeheartedly engaged, not holding anything back. Maybe it is something you are studying or experimenting with, a burning inquiry or need to know. Or it could be something that you want to share through art or words, or a cause that you feel passionate about serving. These are often the things you would do even if you were not getting paid to do them or receiving any external praise.

The soul calls to us in subtle, and sometimes not-so-subtle ways, until we listen. Notice the themes you continually return to, something you deeply want for yourself or for the well-being of others, the things you easily immerse yourself in. Look back on your life and see how your soul has been pulling you forward through your passions and why. Pay close attention to those passions that not only light you up, but benefit others as well. These point toward the purpose you are here to fulfill.

What question have I been living my whole life?

A question is the answer to this question. Like purpose, this may change at different moments of life. But there will be a pervading theme, a continuing narrative thread you can see throughout the experiences you have had in life, the relationships you have been in, and the things you have been drawn toward. Do not rush the answer to this. Allow the inspiration of a quiet mind and a passionate heart to lead you to your truth.

Contemplate the things you believe you were meant to teach others, and the themes that have resonated in your heart year after year. Try to write a clear question about these that represents what your life has been trying to resolve. This core question, the question of your life, is what you have been trying to answer through all of your challenges. Every life has at least one of these, sometimes several. By identifying what your core question is, and who you are in relationship to it, you draw closer to its resolution.

What does my soul want to express?

Being where we need to be, doing what we need to be doing for the greatest impact right now is what living on purpose is all about. You wouldn't be here living and breathing if Spirit didn't want to express something through you today and every day that you are alive. Your life represents a message to the world.

Think about your deeply held core values. Then consider your life in stages: youth, young adulthood, middle age, old age. Determine how well you have expressed these values so far, or not. If you are happy with what you've done with life to this point and what you are spending time, energy, and resources on, then you are probably aligned with your soul's mission. If not, then it is time for some realignment. The universal energy wants to use each one of us for good, if we allow it. Listen. Open. Get out of the way. Let the positive energy flow through you unimpeded.

What is the purpose of life?

Broadening the inquiry from individual purpose to the universal purpose of life is essential if we are to find our peaceful place in it all. Religions and philosophies throughout history have offered many theories and opinions, but we must determine our answer to this in the solitude of our being, to our own satisfaction and no one else's. Only then will we be able to set a strong course and assign meaning to any challenges that try to derail us from our purposeful path.

We must ask this deep question before we are faced with it at the end of life, because without a solid answer, fear will surely be with us both in life and at death. Having a clear perspective on the overall purpose of life helps us clarify *our* unique purpose for being as well. In unification with the one Self, we know both our shared essence and our special role in the field of consciousness.

QUESTION 99

How can I develop greater
trust in my purpose?

To know your purpose is not enough if you cannot act courageously upon it. Fear and doubt will surely derail your best efforts if you do not develop faith in a force greater than your small self, a higher power that can sustain you along the way. Call this what you will, it is the guiding light for your soul, the sustainer and motivator for carrying on when challenges threaten to diminish your sense of purpose.

If you do not currently have a personal relationship with a higher power, spend some time stripping away the beliefs that keep you from this support. Discard any negative or fearful perceptions, any limiting beliefs that others may have instilled in your psyche. Open into a new possibility of wonder and provision from the creative energy that surrounds and sustains us all. Lean into love.

CHAPTER TWELVE

MASTERY

In common modern usage, the word *mastery* refers to proficiency—in a craft, a subject matter, or a physical discipline. In the spiritual realm however, to become a true master means that one is completely unidentified with the personal ego, its agendas, and its desires. This liberated state of being is also called enlightenment, a very rare state to achieve.

As long as we remain in any way driven by a sense of separate self, we are not yet masters. But as we synthesize the wisdom of our heart, mind, body, and soul, we have at least begun the journey home. To arrive requires lifelong discipline, moment-by-moment choosing to forgo the ego-based program for the soul-centered one. This does not mean that everything has to be difficult. It just means we don't shy away from challenge, as it is an integral part of the path toward growth and learning.

Dedicated practice keeps us on the master's path. We must be relentless in observing our thoughts in order to see clearly where we still need to do our spiritual work. We must choose what is right over what is easy and be 100 percent honest with ourselves, impartially analyzing our actions, reactions, motives, and attitudes, so we do not become self-deluded. Introspection prevents us from getting too far off in a negative direction before correcting course.

Regular periods of silence are essential for such deep self-reflection. Through dispassionate inner observation, we can assess our current virtues as well as our shortcomings without developing a superiority or an inferiority complex. If we notice weaknesses or limitations, we can create reminders for ourselves to embody more noble qualities. And when disturbing emotions and urges arise, we can practice not identifying with them as essential truth. Practices such as meditation and prayer keep us centered in truth and love, receptive to intuitive wisdom, and resilient during challenging times.

Vigilance is always necessary. Any thought that takes us away from love, no matter how seemingly trivial or justifiable it may seem, must be thrown out immediately. We can no longer rationalize habits or moods, and all defenses and fear must be exchanged for an unassailable love-based courage. By sticking to the thoughts and actions that take us closer to love, we ally ourselves with truth and with the harmonizing principle of creation.

Mastery is a rigorous path of mindful repetition. It is not the bursts of passionate creativity or brilliant ideas that make a master but rather the daily habits of pure virtue and selflessness. We must stay on the honorable path, regardless of distractions, diversions, or setbacks, because mastery requires nothing less than full passion combined with total surrender.

The measure of our progression toward mastery will be felt in how inwardly content and peaceful we remain regardless of external circumstances, how able we are to create at will what we need, and how anchored we stay in joy and love for all beings. This is the beautiful journey of spiritual awakening.

What soul quality do I need to awaken more?

The Bhagavad Gita is a classic text that illustrates through spiritual metaphor the battle between the ego and the soul that happens in every human life. In it, the soul qualities listed below are named. As you reflect on each one, consider how much you currently embody the quality and how much you would like to. Form a vision of who you wish to become. Be honest with yourself about any undesirable habits or flaws you have. Write down the qualities that will help you overcome these. Choose one of these to apply in diverse ways this week with your family, work, health, and even with your inner self-talk. Find quotes that inspire you or write your own affirmations around the embodiment of this quality. Ask for help or guidance if you need it.

- Fearless
- Pure of heart
- Persevering
- Charitable
- Self-disciplined
- Straightforward
- Peaceful
- Truthful
- Free from wrath
- Compassionate
- Generous
- Gentle
- Humble
- Forgiving
- Patient
- Loving

How does my ego most often try to delude me?

Like recognizing what you don't know, determining how you are being deluded by the ego is a bit tricky. When the ego feels the pressure of being squeezed out of control by the soul, it gets dodgy and camouflages itself in good intentions, praiseworthy efforts, or spiritual pride.

Notice where you feel an edge or a vulnerability right now. This is usually where the ego is hanging out, creating defense strategies and distracting stories. Or it could be where you are still seeking validation or acknowledgment. It may be where anger, fear, or envy are present. By watching your thoughts, words, and actions more closely, you will notice what is causing you to suffer. This is the domain of the ego. Always take notice of whether choices come from your humanity or from your divinity.

Practices such as watching your thoughts, being present, and staying lighthearted, although seemingly simple, novice techniques, are really the way of mastery. Do not be deluded by the ego into thinking you have plumbed the depths of such superficially easy yet fundamentally difficult practices.

Can I be open to everything but attached to nothing?

Notice the moments in which you close down in fear, defensiveness, or attachment to a certain result. Practice open-hearted availability to life as it is occurring in the now and feel the spaciousness that comes from this shift. Notice how your soul can then speak its guidance into this softer space of nonholding.

The more the ego steps back from control into service of the soul, the more generous, at ease, and nonreactive we become. Walking through life with an open heart, available to each moment as it is unfolding and without attachment to a particular outcome, is the ultimate peace. When you flow rather than force, simple solutions arise for even the most complex problems. Let the level of joy and peace you feel in any circumstance be the indicator of your right movement. Feel the connection to the essential joy of your soul bubbling up from within, as you let go, rather than hold tightly to things going a specific way.

What would happen if I let go of the "how" and just followed where joy leads me?

The thinking mind gets very caught up in needing to know *how* certain things are going to happen. It feels more in control when it knows this. But think of a time that you were truly joyous. Most likely you were absorbed in the moment, following a sense of spontaneity rather than any preexisting pressure from the ego and what it thought *should* or *would* occur. As we relinquish the ego-based battle for control, this state of flow arises with ease, and we feel both calm and courageous.

Imagine a life of total joy right now. Really visualize that for a moment, all the details and textures of what that would look like for you. Then notice how the ego tries to limit you through the question of "How can that possibly happen?" Intentionally surrender the need to know *how* your creative vision will occur and lean into the faith that it *can* and *will* as you prioritize joy. Remember, masters take things lightly because they trust.

Who am I?

This is the ultimate question, and one that everyone struggles with on some level. In many ways, before you can begin to answer who you are, you must determine who you are not; un-becoming in order to *be*. It takes vast courage to turn away from the messages you have received from others, labeling you as this or that, and the worldly pressures to be a certain way. If you have accepted someone else's negative commentary on you, then you may think of yourself that way now. Before you can know who you truly are, you must silence these voices that speak anything less than beauty and love about you. Name them as untruths and no longer allow anything or anyone to obscure your true essence.

Worth cannot be earned, and you could never receive enough external validation to prove it, if you don't believe it within your own heart. How you identify yourself is the issue. You are worthy because you are a pure loving soul. Maintain a relentless affirmation of this as you analyze the many layers of your being through the self-reflection process. By embodying full accountability, full functioning, and full awareness, you become actualized and recognize your inherent worth as a spark of Spirit.

How can I be the best version of myself today?

Most days, we look into a mirror to observe our face and body in an effort to look our best out in the world. As we do so, it is important to be self-compassionate as we gaze upon the fragile human form, which ages and sustains injury and disease. Because of the inevitable troubles of being human, always be kind to your physical self, the temple for your soul.

In addition to maintaining the human body vessel, it is even more important to look daily into the mirror of inner self-reflection and to eliminate any disfigurements of anger, fear, sorrow, jealousy, or doubt that plague the mind. Affirm that you are the radiant soul within, untouchable by temporary emotional experiences. Clear away whatever obscures your light. Upon discovery of any shortcoming, cultivate the opposite quality. For reactivity, practice patience. For lethargy, practice enthusiasm. For pride, practice humility. These are the qualities of your true soul nature. In this way, you will ensure the clarity of your inner landscape.

How can I celebrate the mystery of life?

By staying grounded in the sacred now and not draining energy into thoughts of the past or the future, we invite the mystery of life to unveil before us moment by moment. What means nothing in one instant will mean everything in the next. Our job is to release preconceptions and expectations of how we think things should go and revel in the enigmatic nature of just being. The greatest practice is always to remove the obstacles within and around us and then let go into faith and trust.

The ultimate celebration of life and your journey to becoming master of your experience lies in the exceptional ability to transcend fear and to love unconditionally at all times. By aligning with life's principles of harmony and simultaneously celebrating its mystery, you will see the divinity within all circumstances and all beings. Every step you take in this direction is something to celebrate.

Do I choose the light or the darkness?

The story of the light versus the dark is age-old, played out in a million iterations collectively and individually. As we approach mastery, we will be faced repeatedly with this personal choice of allegiance. The dark force, whether it is called temptation, selfishness, Satan, or Maya, strives to undermine our best efforts at personal evolution. And yet, it cannot hold us back from the light of love and peace if we are awake and ready for its tricks.

Stay watchful and notice the energies that pull on you every day and whether you err toward the positive or the negative. Analyze the predominant nature of your thoughts and the trend of your life. Be accountable for your thoughts as well as your actions, aligning them with light. Defend joy, not ignorance. Opt for love, not fear. Practice selflessness. Ask compassionate questions and look at everything as an opportunity to grow and evolve spiritually. In these ways, you will dispel any darkness that may try to dissuade you as you move toward mastery.

What is the most important question
I need to answer right now?

You can't possibly get to your right answers until you have formulated the right questions. So, if the questions you have been asking are not yielding the answers you need, it may be time for a new question. Begin with a short meditation, focusing wholeheartedly on the breath as it occurs naturally. After ten to twenty breaths, allow your focus to soften, witnessing the breath moving spontaneously in and out of the body. Recognize that your physical form is being breathed by some force far greater than you. Say silently to that force, "I am open to hearing the question that is most important for me right now."

When you have identified your most important question, take another moment to consider what the biggest obstacle that might get in your way of answering it might be. Prepare to meet this obstacle as a master would, with strength, courage, willingness, and an endless amount of love.

CONCLUSION

Introspection is a humbling practice, a never-ending process of ego management. It requires that we develop a nonjudgmental awareness in order to see ourselves clearly without getting derailed by self-criticism. It can be exhausting at times as we strip away the qualities and habits that occlude the brilliance of our souls, but as the inner light shines through, it feels so good we want to keep going toward even greater lucidity. Over time, by undertaking all inquiry with a learning mindset, open and willing to explore new paradigms and possibilities, the process can become highly enjoyable.

To persevere as this kind of lifelong learner, rely upon your humor, patience, honesty, and resiliency for effective, ongoing self-reflection. Laugh at your foibles and don't take yourself too seriously. Temporary setbacks happen, and we all slide back into old habits and beliefs that do not serve our highest goals. Don't worry. Just be willing to catch these slips and keep going. As long as you are asking questions, you are growing and evolving. Questions are the art of progress for our souls.

The twelve themes were offered in the order in which I have witnessed people move into conscious change. Use them as guidelines to dip into questions that address what you are currently going through but don't limit yourself to the obvious. They all interweave and overlay upon one another. Here is a review of how the themes of inquiry flow together and encourage personal evolution.

Begin by defining what needs changing. Then identify the core values on which you want to base that change. Call into the light of awareness any negative or limiting beliefs that stand in your way. Be sure you are 100 percent willing to do the work that change requires. As you move forward, recognize the many lessons change brings and practice full accountability for your choices and actions. Accept what is in order to liberate inner space for fresh inspiration to arise. Make time to rest in silence, trusting your intuition so inspiration can become actual knowing. Align your life with truth and love and watch your sense of purpose become clear. If you consistently live all of the above, you are on the path toward mastery.

TIPS AS YOU GO FORWARD

Like cairns on the path toward your truest version of self, often the same questions will arise in your heart in different ways and circumstances. Whether or not you come to a definitive answer, trust in the process of inquiry as it will bring you to inner congruency and put your soul into an interactive dialogue with life.

Set aside time each day for introspection. Find a nice journal to record your reflections and ever-evolving questions. It is also good to keep a pocket notebook or a note on your phone to record questions as they arise spontaneously. Periodically, revisit any questions you resisted. See if you can make friends with them. Analyze the questions life has been throwing your way lately. Ask other people what questions have impacted them or helped them grow. Notice the questions that shape your thinking and that you keep returning to, and how they reflect patterns in your life. Get curious and think, "Isn't this interesting. I wonder . . . ?" Have fun!

If you don't get an answer to a particular question in a reasonable period of time, try reframing it, asking it a different way, or looking for a new layer in what you are trying to solve. When you hit the right wording, it will intuitively click, and it will elicit a response from the divine guide. Between the asking and the response, however, practice surrender. Ask, let go, trust, listen, repeat. Be sure to manage any worries or doubts that arise, as they will only create static in your mind and prevent you from hearing what you need to hear.

The more you embrace internal questions for self-understanding, the more you will want to use them interpersonally as well to strengthen your connection with others. Engaging questions create rapport in social situations, ignite creative solutions, spark innovations, and influence sales in business. Compassionate questions build intimacy in relationships. Inspiring questions, offered at the right time with love and positive intention, are powerful catalysts for transformation.

Let's continue to evolve together, individually and collectively, through conscious introspection and brilliant question asking. In this way, we will all find our way home to love, joy, and our divine oneness.

ACKNOWLEDGMENTS

Greatest gratitude to my husband, Larry, for his support of my calling to write. I could not do it without him. He is my muse, proofreader, cheerleader, massage therapist, breakfast cook, champagne celebrator, comic relief, and all-around dearest love. Thank you, sweetheart, for all that you are and all that you do.

• Deepest appreciation to my son, Benen, for sharing his personal journey of becoming with me. I am so honored to be your mom and so proud of the man you are. Every time I feel you open your heart wider to life and to love, I burst with joy.

• Profound love to my Guru, Paramahansa Yogananda, for helping me to understand the necessity of introspection for spiritual growth. Thank you for the loving lessons in accountability along the way.

• Abundant blessings to all of my clients who so bravely walk the path of personal evolution, trusting me to be their guide. You are my beloved teachers as well as my students.

• High fives to my agent, Steve, who was willing to go against the odds for me.

• A huge hug to my editor, Diana, for sharing my enthusiasm for great questions and for her brilliant editing.

• And finally, to all of my readers, so very much gratitude for taking my words into your hearts. I am humbled by the gift of being able to connect with you in this way.

RECOMMENDED RESOURCES

Adams, Marilee. *Change Your Questions, Change Your Life: 12 Powerful Tools for Leadership, Coaching, and Life*. San Francisco: Berrett-Koehler, 2015.

Aronie, Nancy Slonim. *Writing from the Heart: Tapping the Power of Your Inner Voice*. New York: Hyperion, 1998.

Bach, Richard. *Illusions: The Adventures of a Reluctant Messiah*. New York: Dell, 1977.

Bouanchaud, Bernard. *The Essence of Yoga: Reflections on the Yoga Sutras of Patanjali*. Delhi: Indian Books Centre, 1997.

Brown, Brené. *Dare to Lead: Brave Work. Tough Conversations. Whole Hearts.* New York: Random House, 2018.

———. *Rising Strong as a Spiritual Practice*. Boulder: Sounds True, 2017.

Cameron, Julia. *The Artist's Way: A Spiritual Path to Higher Creativity*. New York: Tarcher, 1992.

Kabat-Zinn, Jon. *Wherever You Go, There You Are: Mindfulness Meditation in Everyday Life*. New York: Hyperion, 1994.

Lindbergh, Anne Morrow. *Gift from the Sea*. Toronto: Pantheon Books, 1975.

McFarlane, Evelyn, and James Saywell. *If . . . Questions for the Soul*. Toronto: Random House, 1998.

Nepo, Mark. *Things That Join the Sea and the Sky: Field Notes on Living*. Boulder: Sounds True, 2017.

Norris, Gunilla. *Inviting Silence: Universal Principles of Meditation*. New York: Bluebridge, 2004.

Rilke, Rainer Maria. *Letters to a Young Poet*. New York: W. W. Norton & Company, 1934.

Ryan, James E. *Wait, What?: And Life's Other Essential Questions*. New York: HarperOne, 2017.

Sinetar, Marsha. *Elegant Choices, Healing Choices*. New York: Paulist Press, 1988.

Singer, Michael. *The Untethered Soul: The Journey Beyond Yourself*. Oakland: New Harbinger, 2007.

Taylor, Elke Elouise. *Change from Within: A Journal of Exercises and Meditations to Transform, Empower, and Reconnect*. New York: Skyhorse, 2017.

Wagamese, Richard. *Embers: One Ojibway's Meditations*. Madeira Park, BC: Douglas & McIntyre, 2016.

Williamson, Marianne. *The Gift of Change: Spiritual Guidance for Living Your Best Life*. New York: HarperCollins, 2004.

Yogananda, Paramahansa. *Autobiography of a Yogi*. Los Angeles: Self-Realization Fellowship, 1998.

———. *In the Sanctuary of the Soul: A Guide to Effective Prayer*. Los Angeles: Self-Realization Fellowship, 1998.

———. *Journey to Self-Realization: Collected Talks and Essays on Realizing God in Daily Life*, vol. 3. Los Angeles: Self-Realization Fellowship, 2005.

ABOUT THE AUTHOR

Jennie Lee is the author of two award-winning books on spiritual living, meditation, and yoga: *Breathing Love: Meditation in Action* and *True Yoga: Practicing with the Yoga Sutras for Happiness & Spiritual Fulfillment*. Her writing has also been featured internationally in magazines such as *Mantra Wellness*, *Light of Consciousness*, *Yoga Therapy Today* and many more. Her essay on the meaning of life was featured in the book *Love* by Nicolae Tanase.

Jennie is a certified yoga therapist (C–IAYT) who is passionate about helping people to create lives filled with purpose and joy. She has been in private practice for over twenty years. In her counseling, she blends the universal ideals and practices of Eastern philosophy with the needs and challenges of modern Western living. Her coaching is based on studies in spiritual psychology, yoga philosophy, and body-centered psychotherapy. The diversity of professionals who have entrusted Jennie with their personal growth speaks to her ability to effectively touch a wide range of individuals. Doctors, lawyers, psychologists, celebrity actors, internationally acclaimed authors, military officers, and more have experienced positive change through working with her.

In addition to individual coaching, she has worked with management groups at corporations such as the World Surf League, National Association of Professional Women, Draper Laboratory, Prudential Locations Realty, and the Jeanne Geiger Crisis Center and has made presentations on yoga, meditation, and mindfulness at studios, schools, and festivals nationwide. When she is not writing or coaching, you will find Jennie surfing in Hawai'i or practicing her Italian in Tuscany. Visit her online at JennieLeeYogaTherapy.com.